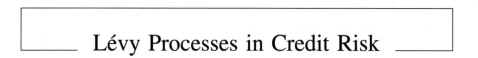

Lévy Processes in Credit Risk

For other titles in the Wiley Finance series
please see www.wiley.com/finance

Lévy Processes in Credit Risk

Wim Schoutens and Jessica Cariboni

A John Wiley and Sons, Ltd., Publication

Library of Congress Cataloging-in-Publication Data:

Schoutens, Wim.
    Levy processes in credit risk/Wim Schoutens and Jessica Cariboni.
        p. cm.
    Includes bibliographical references and index.
    ISBN 978-0-470-74306-5 (cloth)
  1.   Credit–Management–Mathematical models. 2.   Risk management–Mathematical models. 3.   Lévy processes.   I. Cariboni, Jessica.   II. Title.
    HG4026.S337 2009
    658.8'8015195—dc22

                         2009013323

A catalogue record for this book is available from the British Library.

ISBN   978-0-470-74306-5

Typeset in 10/12pt Times by Laserwords Private Limited, Chennai, India.
Printed in Great Britain by TJ International Ltd, Padstow, Cornwall.

To Gabriele and Samuele

Jessica

To Ethel, Jente and Maitzanne

Wim

Contents

Preface

This book introduces Lévy processes in the world of credit risk modelling. Attention is paid to all kind of credit derivatives: from single-name vanillas like Credit Default Swaps (CDSs) to structured credit risk products like Constant Proportion Portfolio Insurances (CPPIs) and Constant Proportion Debt Obligations (CPDOs). It brings in high-tech financial engineering models for the detailed modelling of credit risk instruments. Jumps and extreme events are crucial stylized features and are essential in the modelling of the very volatile credit markets. The credit crunch crisis in the financial markets reconfirmed the need for more refined models. The readers will learn how the classical models (driven by Brownian motions, cf. Black–Scholes settings) can be improved by considering the more flexible class of Lévy processes. By doing this, extreme events and jumps are introduced in the models, leading to a more realistic assessment of the risks present. Besides the setting up of the theoretical framework, much attention will be paid to practical issues. Complex credit derivatives structures (CDOs, CPPIs, CPDOs, etc.) are analysed and illustrated on market data.

Building financial models is very challenging and their application is even more challenging. However, models are just models and are by no means perfect. Models are not the world, they must be seen simply as decision-making tools. Blind belief in any model is extremely dangerous and there is not one right model. A model serves to transform intuitions about the future into a price for a security today. However, that price is just a translation of model assumptions and model inputs.

Moreover, mathematical rigorousness is one thing; implementation is often very time-consuming and asks for many compromises. Getting clean data is another burden. Therefore, special caution has to be taken when applying models to pricing derivatives and it would not harm the financial society to be very humble in applying mathematics in this context of financial markets and derivatives.

All this does not mean that we do not need models at all: we do need models and mathematics, they are just as essential as common sense and experience to make a decision. However, all decision bare some risks. Getting a clue on this risk is actually crucial in making the decision. Knowing where a model is wrong, and how wrong it is, is an essential step in the application of the model itself.

Acknowledgements

The authors want to thank everybody who made this book possible. Special thanks goes to the staff and faculty of the Mathematics Department of the Catholic University of Leuven, the EURANDOM Institute and the Joint Research Centre of the European Commission in Ispra. We would like to thank also many colleagues in academia as well as in the industry for their support, interest and valuable comments.

The authors also thank the staff at John Wiley & Sons, Ltd, for making all this possible and for their warm collaboration.

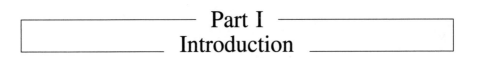

Part I
Introduction

1
An Introduction to Credit Risk

1.1 CREDIT RISK

In general terms, credit risk refers to the risk that a specified reference entity does not meet its credit obligations within a specified time horizon T. If this happens, we say that a default event has occurred.

Credit risk is present in everyday life. For instance, consider a person who goes to a bank and asks for a loan to buy a house; suppose the loan is granted by the bank, which agrees with the person that the money will be paid back following certain criteria and within a predetermined time period. In this situation the credit institution is exposed to the risk that this person will not be able to repay (part of) the loan, or will not meet the criteria established. The type of risk the bank is facing is exactly credit risk: the reference entity is the person who asks for the loan; default occurs on the day the creditor declares that he is not able to honour his obligations.

This simple example shows the main characteristics of credit risk. We can see that two sides are involved: on one hand the bank, which is exposed to the risk; on the other the reference entity – sometimes called the *obligor* – who has to fulfil a series of obligations. Further, there is a set of criteria that defines how these obligations have to be met, i.e. a set of criteria that identifies the default of the entity. Finally, the risk is spread over a determined time length $[0, T]$, where T is often referred to as the *maturity* or the *time horizon*. Moreover, the example shows that there are various elements that the bank does not know on the day it grants the loan. First, the bank does not know the probability that the default will actually occur. Banks try to overcome this problem by collecting information about the person who is asking for the loan in order to get a flavour of the probability that the person will not be able to repay the money. Hypothesizing that default will occur, it is uncertain when this will happen. Also, the severity of the loss is indefinite.

In finance, life is a bit more complicated, but credit risk can always be characterized in terms of these components: the obligor, the set of criteria defining default, and the time interval over which the risk is spread. Often, instead of dealing with persons and loans, one deals with companies and bonds. In this case default can be defined in a variety of ways. Besides the complete financial bankruptcy of the reference entity, other examples of default can be the failure to pay an obligation (e.g. the coupon of a bond), a rating downgrade of the company, its restructuring, or a merger with another corporation. It is sufficient to switch on the TV to understand that default events are quite rare but have a strong impact on financial markets. Every day rating agencies such as Moody's and Standard & Poor evaluate the creditworthiness of hundreds of companies traded on the market. A change in the rating of a company will affect the prices of all related financial instruments, such as spreads of corporate bonds.

Credit risk thus affects the profits and losses of thousands of billions of euros invested every day by banks in financial portfolios, grouping together baskets of reference entities that might jointly default within the same time horizon. It is clear that in this case there is an additional element to be taken into consideration, which is the joint default probability distribution of portfolio components. Multiple defaults are extremely rare events that can be driven, for instance, by natural catastrophes, systemic defaults, political events, terrorist episodes, or caused by the complex linked-structure of the capital market.

Following the Basel Accord (2004), banks have to set aside a certain amount of capital to cover the risk inherent in their credit portfolios. Subject to certain minimum conditions and disclosure requirements, the Basel II Accord allows credit institutions to rely on their own internal estimates of risk components, which determine the capital requirements to cover credit risk. The risk components include measures of the probability of default, the recovery rate and the exposure at default. This has, of course, encouraged banks to invest in modelling credit risk with more and more sophisticated approaches. Banks have also a second option to mitigate their credit risk: they can hedge credit risk by buying credit derivatives. The Basel II Accord also provides the inclusion of credit risk mitigation techniques to assess the overall risk of a credit portfolio.

1.1.1 Historical and Risk-Neutral Probabilities

The main objective of the present book is to build advanced models to price different kinds of financial instruments whose price is related to the probability that a default event will occur or not between time 0 and time t ($0 \leq t \leq T$, T being the maturity) for a reference entity or a bunch of reference entities.

In mathematical finance, there are two important probability measures: a historical and a risk-neutral (or pricing) measure. The historical probability of an event is the probability that this event happens in reality (in the so-called real world). The risk-neutral measure is an artificial measure: The risk-neutral probability of an event is the probability that one uses to value (by so-called risk-neutral valuation techniques) derivatives contracts depending on the event. Since we are dealing in this book with the valuation of credit derivatives contracts, the measure of interest to us will be the risk-neutral measure. More precisely, the risk-neutral valuation principle states that the price of a derivative is given by the expected value under the risk-neutral measure of the discounted payoff:

Price = $\mathbb{E}$ [Discounted payoff].

In our framework – the valuation of credit derivatives contracts – we are interested in identifying the proper risk-neutral probability.

Throughout the book, the risk-neutral probability that a default event will not occur between time 0 and time t for a single-reference entity will be referred to as *survival probability*:

$$P_{\text{Surv}}(t) = \text{Probability that default will not occur in } [0, t]. \tag{1.1}$$

Correspondingly, we will call *default probability* the risk-neutral probability that the obligor does actually default between 0 and t:

$$P_{\text{Def}}(t) = \text{Probability that default will occur in } [0, t]. \tag{1.2}$$

Clearly for each $0 \leq t \leq T$, we will have that $P_{\text{Def}}(t) = 1 - P_{\text{Surv}}(t)$.

Although, as mentioned above, we will almost always work with risk-neutral probabilities, one can also get a flavour of the historical default probabilities observed in the market. Figure 1.1 shows the average 1-year default rates for the period 1983–2000 by rating classes, following Moody's classification. Each bar represents the average over the sample period of the fraction of companies defaulted in 1 year in each rating class.

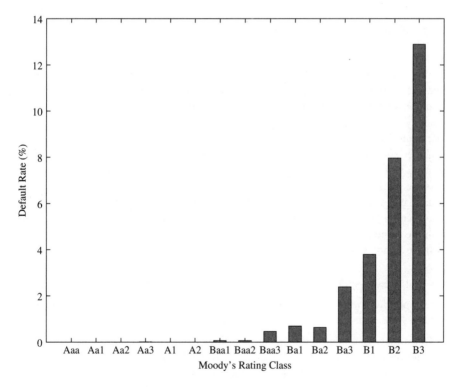

Figure 1.1 Historical average 1-year default rate for 1983–2000 following Moody's classification. *Source:* Moody's, in Duffie and Singleton (2003)

In the multivariate setting, the (risk-neutral) probability that more defaults occur within the time horizon needs to be estimated. Consider, for simplicity, two obligors, i and j. The joint (risk-neutral) survival and default probabilities are defined as:

$$P_{\text{Surv}}^{ij}(t) = \text{Probability that both obligors } i, j \text{ will not default in } [0, t]$$

$$P_{\text{Def}}^{ij}(t) = \text{Probability that both obligors } i, j \text{ will default in } [0, t].$$

If the two obligors are independent, we have that

$$P_{\text{Surv}}^{ij}(t) = P_{\text{Surv}}^{i}(t) \cdot P_{\text{Surv}}^{j}(t)$$

$$P_{\text{Def}}^{ij}(t) = P_{\text{Def}}^{i}(t) \cdot P_{\text{Def}}^{j}(t).$$

However, market data provides evidence that the hypothesis of independence does not hold. The dependence structure among obligors relates to the fact that they live in the same global market, and often financial/commercial relationships exist among companies.

1.1.2 Bond Prices and Default Probability

Bond traders have developed procedures for taking credit risk into account when pricing corporate bonds. They collect market data on actively traded bonds to calculate a generic zero-coupon yield curve for each credit rating category. These zero-coupon yield curves are then used to value other corporate bonds. For example, a newly issued A-rated bond will be priced using the zero-coupon yield curve calculated from other A-rated bonds.

Under specific assumptions, if the yield curve of a risk-free zero-coupon bond and the yield curve of a corporate bond with the same maturity are known, it is possible to estimate the default probability of the corporation issuing the corporate bond. Let us indicate with $y^*(T)$ and $y(T)$ respectively the yield on a corporate zero-coupon bond with maturity T and the yield on a risk-free zero-coupon bond with the same maturity. Considering a principal $F = 100$, the values at time $t = 0$ of these bonds will thus be, respectively:

$$100 \exp(-y(T)T) = 100 B_0(T)$$

$$100 \exp(-y^*(T)T) = 100 B_0^*(T).$$

To estimate risk-neutral default probabilities from these bond prices, we assume that the present value of the cost of default equals the excess of the price of the risk-free bond over the price of the corporate bond:

$$100(B_0(T) - B_0^*(T)) = 100(\exp(-y(T)T) - \exp(-y^*(T)T)).$$

This means that the higher yield on a corporate bond is entirely the compensation for possible losses from default. Note that this is only an approximation, since other factors, such as liquidity, also influence the spread.

If we assume that there is no recovery in the event of default, the calculation of the default probability $P_{\text{Def}}(T)$ is relatively easy. In fact there is a probability $P_{\text{Def}}(T)$ that the corporate bond will be worth zero at maturity and a probability of $(1 - P_{\text{Def}}(T))$ that it will be worth 100. This means that (by risk-neutral valuation)

$$100B_0^*(T) = B_0(T)(P_{\text{Def}}(T) \times 0 + (1 - P_{\text{Def}}(T)) \times 100)$$
$$= B_0(T)100(1 - P_{\text{Def}}(T)).$$

Hence, we can estimate the risk-neutral default probability as:

$$P_{\text{Def}}(T) = \frac{B_0(T) - B_0^*(T)}{B_0(T)}$$
$$= 1 - \exp(-(y^*(T) - y(T))T).$$

For example, suppose that the spread over the risk-free rate for a 5-year and a 10-year BBB-rated zero-coupon bond are 130 and 170 bps, respectively, and that there is no recovery in the event of default, then:

$$P_{\text{Def}}(5) = 1 - \exp(-0.0130 \times 5) = 0.0629;$$
$$P_{\text{Def}}(10) = 1 - \exp(-0.0170 \times 10) = 0.1563.$$

It also follows that the (risk-neutral) probability of default between 5 years and 10 years is $0.0934(= 0.1563 - 0.0629)$.

This analysis assumes no recovery on bonds in the event of a default. In reality, when a company goes bankrupt, entities that are owed money by the company file claims against the assets of the company. The assets are sold by the liquidator and the proceeds are used to meet the claims as far as possible. Some claims typically have priorities over others and are met more fully. We define the *recovery rate* as the proportion of the claimed amount received in the event of a default. Historical data on the amounts recovered show that senior secured debtholders received an average around 50% while junior subordinated debtholders received around 20% per par value.

If we relax the hypothesis of zero recovery rate and we suppose a positive expected recovery rate of $0 \leq R \leq 1$, then, in the event of default the bondholder receives a proportion R of the bond's no-default value. Going back to the example above we will have that:

- If there is no default, the bondholder receives 100. The bond's no-default present value is $100B_0(T)$ and the probability of no-default is $P_{\text{Surv}}(T) = (1 - P_{\text{Def}}(T))$.
- If a default occurs, the bondholder receives $100R$. The bond's default present value is thus $100RB_0(T)$ and the probability of default is $P_{\text{Def}}(T)$.

- The value of the bond is therefore:

$$100B_0^*(T) = B_0(T)(P_{\text{Def}}(T) \times 100R + (1 - P_{\text{Def}}(T)) \times 100).$$

This gives

$$
\begin{aligned}
P_{\text{Def}}(T) &= \frac{B_0(T) - B_0^*(T)}{(1 - R)B_0(T)} \\
&= \frac{1 - \exp(-(y^*(T) - y(T))T)}{1 - R}.
\end{aligned}
$$

For example, going back to the example above, if we suppose that the spread over the risk-free rate for a 5-year and a 10-year BBB-rated zero-coupon bond are 130 and 170 bps, respectively, and there is a recovery rate of 50%, then:

$$P_{\text{Def}}(5) = \frac{1 - \exp(-0.0130 \times 5)}{1 - 0.5} = 0.1258;$$

$$P_{\text{Def}}(10) = \frac{1 - \exp(-0.0170 \times 10)}{1 - 0.5} = 0.3126.$$

It also follows that the probability of default between 5 years and 10 years is $0.1868(= 0.3126 - 0.1258)$.

1.2   CREDIT RISK MODELLING

Modern finance has put much effort into developing new models for credit risk. There are a number of reasons related to this growth of interest in credit risk. On the one hand, the volumes traded on the market of financial instruments related to credit risk have increased exponentially in recent years (see also Section 1.3); on the other hand, as already mentioned in Section 1.1, the implementation of the Basel II Accord has encouraged financial institutions to develop in-house models to assess their credit exposure. Credit risk models are usually classified into two categories: structural models and intensity-based models.

Structural models – known also as *firm-value* models – link an event of default to the value of the financial assets[1] of the firm. In general, the dynamics of the asset value $V = \{V_t, 0 \le t \le T\}$ is given and an event of default is defined in terms of boundary conditions on this process. For instance, let us introduce the following simple structural model. We consider a single reference and hypothesize that default happens if its asset value falls below a fixed level L within the time horizon, as shown in Figure 1.2. For sake of illustration, it is assumed that the asset value follows a geometric Brownian motion with drift $\mu = 0.05$ and standard deviation

---

[1] Throughout the book the terms 'value of the financial assets' and 'asset value' will be used interchangeably.

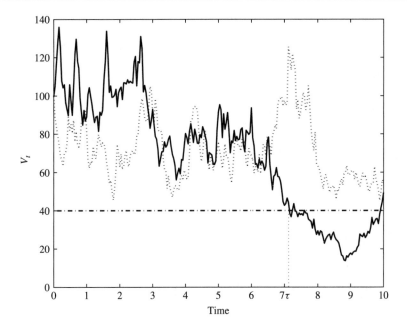

Figure 1.2 Example of structural model ($T = 10$ years) where the dynamics of the asset value, V_t is a geometric Brownian motions ($\mu = 0.05$, $\sigma = 0.4$). The default barrier level is represented by the line $L = 40$. If the scenario represented by the solid line occurs, the obligor will default; if V_t follows the dotted line, the obligor will survive

$\sigma = 0.4$ (for details on how to generate the path, see also Section 2.1 of Chapter 2). It is furthermore assumed that the asset value at time $t = 0$ is $V_0 = 100$ and the level L, represented by the dash-dot line in Figure 1.2, equals 40. The plot shows that, depending on the evolution of V, the reference asset may survive (dotted line), or a default event can occur (solid line). Figure 1.2 also shows that if the asset value follows the solid path, default will occur after around 7 years.

A large number of various firm-value approaches have been developed since the 1970s; Chapter 4 presents a general introduction of the most important structural approaches, highlighting their advantages and shortcomings. Subsequently it introduces structural models for credit risk where the asset value is assumed to follow one of the Lévy processes described in Chapter 2.

Intensity-based models, known also as *hazard rate* or *reduced-form* models, focus directly on modelling the default probability. The basic idea lies in the fact that at any instant there is a probability that an obligor will default, which depends on its overall *health*. Default is defined at the first jump of a counting process $N = \{N_t, 0 \leq t \leq T\}$ with intensity $\lambda = \{\lambda_t, 0 \leq t \leq T\}$, which thus determines the price of credit risk. Figure 1.3 shows that the higher the default intensity, the higher the probability of a default event. In fact, the intensity – which can be deterministic or stochastic – models the default rate for the reference entity. Let us

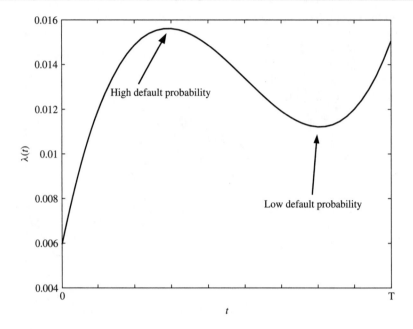

Figure 1.3 Deterministic intensity rate of default. The behaviour of the intensity over time describes the *health* of the reference entity

assume that the reference entity has survived up to time t and let us indicate with τ the default time. The intensity of default is defined as:

$$\lambda_t = \lim_{h \to 0} \frac{\mathbb{P}(t < \tau \le t + h | \tau > t)}{h},$$

where $\mathbb{P}$ is the probability measure. This equation tells us that, roughly speaking, for a small time interval $\Delta t > 0$:

$$\mathbb{P}(\tau \le t + \Delta t | \tau > t) \approx \lambda_t \Delta t.$$

A classical example of counting process is the (homogeneous) Poisson process with constant default intensity $\lambda > 0$ (see Section 2.3.1 of Chapter 2). For this process, the probability that the counting process $N = \{N_t, 0 \le t \le T\}$ equals an integer n is given by the Poisson distribution:

$$\mathbb{P}(N_t = n) = \exp(-\lambda t) \frac{(\lambda t)^n}{n!}.$$

A corresponding default model was developed by Jarrow and Turnbull (1995). Under this model the probability of surviving from 0 to t is given by

$$P_{\text{Surv}}(t) = \mathbb{P}(N_t = 0) = \exp(-\lambda t).$$

Due to the properties of the Poisson distribution, the expected time of the first jump of $N = \{N_t, 0 \leq t \leq T\}$ – i.e. the expected time of default – is given by[2] $1/\lambda$. For example, at a constant default intensity of $\lambda = 0.1$, the probability of default in 5 years is around 9.52%, and the expected time of default is 10 years.

Chapter 5 briefly reviews the intensity-based models available in the literature and focuses on jump-driven default intensity models. The class of Ornstein–Uhlenbeck (OU) processes driven by Lévy processes is assumed to describe the dynamics of the default intensity over time.

We will see that, from a fundamental point of view, it is important to have jumps in the intensity regime or in the firm-value price process because changes in the creditworthiness (default intensity or firm-value) are often shock driven: sudden events in reality cause important changes on the view on the company's probability of default. Standard examples of such dramatic changes in the regime are discovery of fraud (e.g. Parmalat), a reviewing of company's results, default of a competitor, a terroristic attack, etc.

1.3   CREDIT DERIVATIVES

Credit derivatives are derivatives whose payoffs are affected by the default of a specified reference entity (or to a basket of reference entities). As introduced in Section 1.1, in many cases credit derivatives are used to hedge, transfer or manage credit risk and can be thought of as an insurance against default. The idea is that credit risk is transferred without reallocating the ownership of the underlying asset. In general, two counterparties are involved: the *protection buyer* and the *protection seller*, which agree on a contract related to the default of the reference entity(ies). The market for credit derivatives was created in the early 1990s in London and New York. Since then, diverse and complex products have been rising, thus stimulating the development of the credit derivatives market. Figure 1.4 shows the growth of the volumes of credit derivatives exchanged on the market from 1997, testifying to the exponential popularity of these products. It also compares the credit derivative market with the market for cash bonds.

Banks and investments undertakings have contributed in fostering the growth of the credit derivatives market both for money-making purposes and to mitigate the capital requirements imposed by the Basel II Accord. Indeed, banks use credit derivatives to hedge or assume credit risk, to enhance portfolio diversification, and to improve the management of their portfolios.

A big share of the derivatives market is taken up by Credit Default Swaps (CDSs), which are designed to isolate the risk of default on credit obligations. A lot of other types of credit instruments exist, among which the most important are credit spread products, such as forwards and constant maturity swaps. When considering multivariate instruments (i.e. instruments based on more than one reference entity),

---

[2] For a Poisson distribution with constant intensity λ, the time between two consecutive jumps is Gamma$(1, \lambda)$ distributed (or equivalently Exponential(λ) distributed). The average time between two consecutive jumps is thus $1/\lambda$.

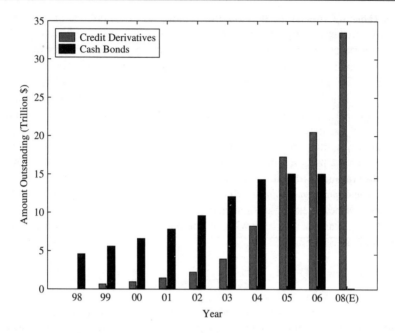

Figure 1.4 Global credit derivatives and cash bonds outstandings, in trillions of US dollars. *Source:* British Bankers Association, JP Morgan Research

Table 1.1 Shares of the market for different classes of credit derivatives in 2004 and 2006. *Source:* British Bankers Association, JP Morgan Research

Type	2004	2006
Single-Name CDSs	51.0%	32.9%
Full Index Names	9.0%	30.1%
Synthetic CDOs	16.0%	16.3%
Tranched Index Trades	2.0%	7.6%
Credit-Linked Notes	6.0%	3.1%
Others	16.0%	10.0%

the most famous are Collateralized Loan Obligations (CLOs), and Collateralized Debt Obligations (CDOs). Recently also instruments based on indices of credit derivatives have become quite popular. Table 1.1 presents the shares of the market of the most important classes of credit derivatives for 2004 and 2006. An overview of credit derivatives and credit-linked notes can be found for instance in Das (2000).

Over the last few years the profiles of market players have evolved and modified substantially along with the credit derivatives market itself. Table 1.2 shows that the credit derivatives are mostly used by banks for trading activities and to hedge loan portfolios. Other important players are hedge funds.

Table 1.2 Shares of the market market players. *Source:* British Bankers Association, JP Morgan Research

Type	Protection buyers	Protection sellers
Bank's Trading Activities	35%	39%
Full Index Banks-Loan Portfolio	9%	20%
Hedge Funds	32%	28%
Pension Funds	4%	2%
Corporates	1%	2%
Mono-line Insurers	8%	2%
Re-Insurers	4%	2%
Other Insurers	5%	2%
Mutual Funds	3%	2%
Other	1%	1%

1.4 MODELLING ASSUMPTIONS

1.4.1 Probability Space and Filtrations

We assume a fixed finite planning horizon T. Let us denote by Ω the set of all possible outcomes in which we are interested. Next, we will set up a mathematical system to describe the flow of information. $\mathcal{F}$ is a sigma-algebra (a family of subsets of Ω closed under any countable collection of set operations) containing all sets for which we want to make a statement; $\mathbb{P}$ gives the probability that an event in such a set of $\mathcal{F}$ will happen.

Moreover, we equip our probability space $(\Omega, \mathcal{F}, \mathbb{P})$ with a *filtration*. A filtration is a non-decreasing family $\mathbb{F} = (\mathcal{F}_t, 0 \leq t \leq T)$ of sub-σ-fields of $\mathcal{F}$: $\mathcal{F}_s \subset \mathcal{F}_t \subset \mathcal{F}_T \subset \mathcal{F}$ for $0 \leq s < t \leq T$; here $\mathcal{F}_t$ represents the information available at time t, and the filtration $\mathbb{F} = (\mathcal{F}_t, 0 \leq t \leq T)$ represents the information flow evolving with time.

In general, we assume that the *filtered probability space* $(\Omega, \mathcal{F}, \mathbb{P}, \mathbb{F})$ satisfies the 'usual conditions':

(a) $\mathcal{F}$ is $\mathbb{P}$-complete.
(b) $\mathcal{F}_0$ contains all $\mathbb{P}$-null sets of Ω. This means intuitively that we know which events are possible and which are not.
(c) $\mathbb{F}$ is right-continuous, i.e. $\mathcal{F}_t = \cap_{s > t} \mathcal{F}_s$; a technical condition.

In this context, we assume that filtrations we work with are sufficiently rich that everything we need to measure we can measure, especially functionals of the underlying Lévy processes (see also Bingham and Kiesel 1998).

A *stochastic process* $X = \{X_t, 0 \leq t \leq T\}$ is a family of random variables defined on a complete probability space $(\Omega, \mathcal{F}, \mathbb{P})$. We say X is adapted to the filtration $\mathbb{F}$ or just $\mathbb{F}$-*adapted*, if X_t is $\mathcal{F}_t$-measurable (we denote this by $X_t \in \mathcal{F}_t$) for each t: thus X_t is known at time t.

We say that X is $\mathbb{F}$-*predictable* if $X_t \in \mathcal{F}_{t-} = \bigcup_{s<t} \mathcal{F}_s$ (i.e. X_t is $\mathcal{F}_{t-}$-measurable) for each t: thus X_t is known strictly before time t.

Starting with a stochastic process X on the probability space $(\Omega, \mathcal{F}, \mathbb{P})$, we call $\mathbb{F}^X = \{\mathcal{F}_t^X, 0 \leq t \leq T\}$ the natural filtration of X, i.e. the 'smallest' filtration containing all information that can be observed if we watch X evolving through time.

Learning During the Flow of Time

The 'filtration' concept is not very easy to understand. In order to clarify this a little, we explain the idea of filtration in a very idealized situation. We will consider a stochastic process X which starts at some value, zero say. It will remain there until $t = 1$, at which time it can jump with positive probability to the value a or to a different value b. The process will stay at that value until $t = 2$ at which time it will jump again with positive probability to two different values: c and d, say, if the process was at time $t = 1$ at state a, and f and g say if the process was at time $t = 1$ at state b. From then on the process will stay in the same value. The universum of the probability space consists of all possible paths the process can follow, i.e. all possible outcomes of the experiment. We will denote the path $0 \to a \to c$ by ω_1; similarly the paths $0 \to a \to d, 0 \to b \to f$ and $0 \to b \to g$ are denoted by ω_2, ω_3 and ω_4 respectively. So we have $\Omega = \{\omega_1, \omega_2, \omega_3, \omega_4\}$. We set here $\mathcal{F} = \mathcal{D}(\Omega)$, the set of all subsets of Ω.

In this situation, the natural filtration of X will be the following flow of information:

$$\mathcal{F}_t = \{\emptyset, \Omega\} \qquad\qquad\qquad 0 \leq t < 1;$$
$$\mathcal{F}_t = \{\emptyset, \Omega, \{\omega_1, \omega_2\}, \{\omega_3, \omega_4\}\} \quad 1 \leq t < 2;$$
$$\mathcal{F}_t = \mathcal{D}(\Omega) = \mathcal{F} \qquad\qquad 2 \leq t \leq T.$$

To each of the filtrations given above, we associate respectively the following partitions (i.e. the finest possible one) of Ω:

$$\mathcal{P}_0 = \{\Omega\} \qquad\qquad\qquad 0 \leq t < 1;$$
$$\mathcal{P}_1 = \{\{\omega_1, \omega_2\}, \{\omega_3, \omega_4\}\} \qquad 1 \leq t < 2;$$
$$\mathcal{P}_2 = \{\{\omega_1\}, \{\omega_2\}, \{\omega_3\}, \{\omega_4\}\} \quad 2 \leq t \leq T.$$

At time $t = 0$ we only know that some event $\omega \in \Omega$ will happen; at time $t = 2$ we will know which event $\omega^* \in \Omega$ has happened. So at times $0 \leq t < 1$ we only know that there will be some event $\omega^* \in \Omega$. At time points after $t = 1$ and strictly before $t = 2$, i.e. $1 \leq t < 2$, we know the state to which the process has jumped at time $t = 1$: a or b. So at that time we will know the particular set of $\mathcal{P}_1$ to which ω^* will belong: it will belong to $\{\omega_1, \omega_2\}$ if we jumped at time $t = 1$ to a and to $\{\omega_3, \omega_4\}$ if we jumped to b. Finally, at time $t = 2$, we will know the particular set of $\mathcal{P}_2$ to which ω^* will belong, in other words we will know then the complete path of the process.

During the flow of time we thus learn about the partitions. Having the information $\mathcal{F}_t$ revealed is equivalent to knowing the particular set of the partition to which the event ω^* belongs that time. The partitions become finer in each step, and thus information on ω^* becomes more detailed.

1.4.2 The Risk-Free Asset

Throughout the book, we will make use of the so-called *discounting factor* to price the various types of credit derivatives taken into consideration. This section aims to introduce the notation adopted for this factor.

Definition 1.1 (Risk-Free Asset)   *The price process $B = \{B_t, 0 \leq t \leq T\}$ is the price of a risk-free asset if it follows the dynamics*

$$\mathrm{d}B_t = r_t B_t \,\mathrm{d}t \tag{1.3}$$

where $r = \{r_t, 0 \leq t \leq T\}$ is called the short rate and can be either an adapted process or a deterministic function of time.

From now on we will indicate with $D(t, T)$ the ratio:

$$D(t, T) = \mathbb{E}\left[\frac{B_t}{B_T}\right], \tag{1.4}$$

where $\mathbb{E}$ is the expected value operator. $D(t, T)$ is strictly related with the price of bonds: indeed it can be thought of as the price at time t of a default-free zero-coupon bond with maturity T and face value 1.

In the case where $r = \{r_t, 0 \leq t \leq T\}$ is a stochastic process, the discounting factor becomes, using Equation (1.3).

$$D(t, T) = \mathbb{E}\left[\exp\left(-\int_t^T r_s \,\mathrm{d}s\right)\right]. \tag{1.5}$$

If we suppose the short rate to be a deterministic function of time, Equation (1.3) shows that there is no stochastic component in the dynamics of $B = \{B_t, 0 \leq t \leq T\}$, i.e. there is a complete knowledge of the risk-free asset dynamics by simply observing the actual short rate r_t. It results in this case that the discounting factor is:

$$D(t, T) = \exp\left(-\int_t^T r_s \,\mathrm{d}s\right). \tag{1.6}$$

Finally, if we interpret the risk-free asset as a bank account with a short rate of constant interest r, we have that:

$$D(t, T) = \exp\left(-r(T - t)\right). \tag{1.7}$$

2
An Introduction to Lévy Processes

2.1 BROWNIAN MOTION

The Normal distribution, $N(\mu, \sigma^2)$, is one of the most important distributions in many research areas. It lives on the real line, has mean $\mu \in \mathbb{R}$ and variance $\sigma^2 > 0$. Its density function is given as

$$f_N(x; \mu, \sigma^2) = \frac{1}{\sqrt{2\pi\sigma^2}} \exp\left(-\frac{(x-\mu)^2}{2\sigma^2}\right).$$

In Figure 2.1, one sees the typical bell-shaped curve of the density of a Standard Normal density $N(0, 1)$ and of a Normal distribution $N(0, 2)$. As can be seen in Table 2.1, the Normal (μ, σ^2) distribution is symmetric around its mean, and always has a kurtosis equal to 3.

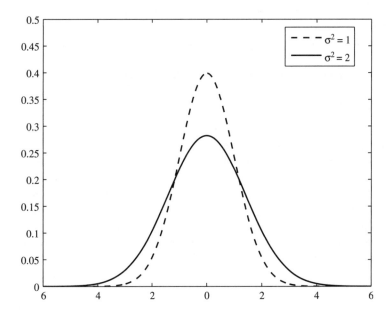

Figure 2.1 Probability density function of a Standard Normal distribution $N(0, 1)$ and of a Normal distribution $N(0, 2)$

Table 2.1 Moments of the
Normal distribution $N(\mu, \sigma^2)$

	$N(\mu, \sigma^2)$
Mean	μ
Variance	σ^2
Skewness	0
Kurtosis	3

We will denote by

$$\Phi(x) = \int_{-\infty}^{x} f_N(u; 0, 1)\, du \tag{2.1}$$

the distribution function for a random variable X that is Standard Normally distributed (i.e. $X \sim N(0, 1)$).

Definition 2.1 (Brownian Motion) *A stochastic process $W = \{W_t, t \geq 0\}$ is a Brownian motion (or Wiener process) if the following conditions hold:*

1. $W_0 = 0$.
2. *The process has stationary increments, i.e. the distribution of the increment $W_{t+s} - W_t$ over the interval $[t, t + s]$ does not depend on t, but only on the length s of the interval.*
3. *The process has independent increments, i.e. if $l < s \leq t < u$, $W_u - W_t$ and $W_s - W_l$ are independent random variables. In other words, increments over non-overlapping time intervals are stochastically independent.*
4. *For $0 \leq s < t$ the random variable $W_t - W_s$ follows a Normal distribution $N(0, t - s)$.*

The paths of a Brownian motion are continuous but very erratic. In fact it can be demonstrated that they are of infinite variation on any compact time interval.[1] Finally, the following scaling property holds: if $W = \{W_t, t \geq 0\}$ is a Brownian motion then for any $c \neq 0$, $\hat{W} = \{\hat{W}_t = cW_{t/c^2}, t \geq 0\}$ is also a Brownian motion.

A Brownian motion can be easily simulated by discretizing time using a very small step Δt. The value of a Brownian motion at time points $\{n\Delta t, n = 1, 2, \ldots\}$ is obtained by sampling a series of Standard Normal $N(0, 1)$ random numbers $\{v_n, n = 1, 2, \ldots\}$ and setting:

$$W_0 = 0, \quad W_{n\Delta t} = W_{(n-1)\Delta t} + \sqrt{\Delta t}\, v_n.$$

Figure 2.2 shows a typical Brownian motion path.

---

[1] For a definition see, for example, Sato (1999)

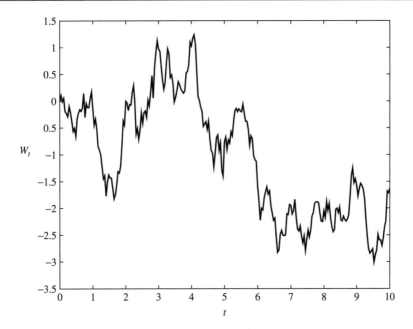

Figure 2.2   A sample path of a Brownian motion

Geometric Brownian motion, which is constructed out of a Brownian motion, is one of the most popular processes in finance, e.g. it is the basis of the Black–Scholes model for stock price dynamics in continuous time. A stochastic process $S = \{S_t, t \geq 0\}$ is a geometric Brownian motion if it satisfies the following stochastic differential equation

$$dS_t = S_t(\mu\, dt + \sigma\, dW_t), \quad S_0 > 0, \tag{2.2}$$

where $W = \{W_t, t \geq 0\}$ is a standard Brownian motion, μ is the so-called drift parameter, and $\sigma > 0$ is the volatility parameter. Equation (2.2) has the unique solution (see, for instance, Björk 1998):

$$S_t = S_0 \exp\left(\left(\mu - \frac{\sigma^2}{2}\right)t + \sigma W_t\right).$$

The related log-returns

$$\log S_t - \log S_0 = \left(\mu - \frac{\sigma^2}{2}\right)t + \sigma W_t$$

follow a Normal distribution, $N(t(\mu - \sigma^2/2), \sigma^2 t)$. Thus S has a *Lognormal* distribution. Figure 2.3 shows the realization of the geometric Brownian motion based on the sample path of the standard Brownian motion of Figure 2.2 with $S_0 = 100$, $\mu = 0.05$ and $\sigma^2 = 0.3$.

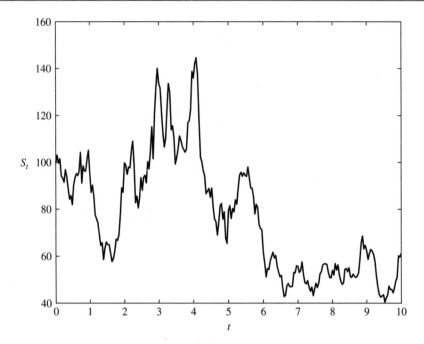

Figure 2.3   A sample path of a geometric Brownian motion with $S_0 = 100$, $\mu = 0.05$ and $\sigma^2 = 0.3$. The corresponding Brownian motion is represented in Figure 2.2

2.2   LÉVY PROCESSES

Definition 2.2 (*Characteristic Function*)   *The characteristic function ϕ of a distribution – or equivalently of a random variable X – is the Fourier–Stieltjes transform of the distribution function $F(x) = \mathbb{P}(X \leq x)$:*

$$\phi_X(u) = \mathbb{E}\left[\exp\left(iuX\right)\right] = \int_{-\infty}^{\infty} \exp\left(iux\right) \, dF(x), \tag{2.3}$$

where i *is the imaginary number* ($i^2 = -1$).

In almost all cases we will work with a random variable X that has a continuous distribution with density function, say $f_X(x)$. In this case Equation (2.3) becomes:

$$\phi_X(u) = \mathbb{E}[\exp(iuX)] = \int_{-\infty}^{+\infty} \exp(iux) f_X(x) \, dx.$$

The most important property of the characteristic function is that for any random variable X, it always exists, it is continuous, and it determines X univocally.

Moreover, for independent variables X and Y:

$$\phi_{X+Y}(u) = \phi_X(u)\phi_Y(u). \qquad (2.4)$$

Example The characteristic function of the Normal distribution $N(\mu, \sigma^2)$ is given by

$$\phi_N(u) = \int_{-\infty}^{+\infty} \exp(iux) \frac{1}{\sqrt{2\pi\sigma^2}} \exp\left(-\frac{(x-\mu)^2}{2\sigma^2}\right) dx$$

$$= \exp(iu\mu) \exp\left(-\frac{1}{2}\sigma^2 u^2\right). \qquad (2.5)$$

The following are some of the functions, related to the characteristic function, that often appear in the literature:

- The cumulant function:

$$k(u) = \log \mathbb{E}[\exp(-uX)] = \log \phi(iu).$$

- The moment-generating function:

$$\vartheta(u) = \mathbb{E}[\exp(uX)] = \phi(-iu).$$

- The cumulant characteristic function, often called the characteristic exponent:

$$\psi(u) = \log \mathbb{E}[\exp(iuX)] = \log \phi(u),$$

or equivalently

$$\phi(u) = \exp(\psi(u)). \qquad (2.6)$$

Definition 2.3 (Infinitely Divisible Distribution) *Suppose $\phi(u)$ is the characteristic function of a random variable X. If, for every positive integer n, $\phi(u)$ is also the nth power of a characteristic function, we say that the distribution is infinitely divisible.*

In terms of X this means that one could write for any n:

$$X = Y_1^{(n)} + \cdots + Y_n^{(n)},$$

where $Y_i^{(n)}$, $i = 1, \ldots, n$, are independent identically distributed (i.i.d.) random variables, all following a law with characteristic function $\phi(z)^{1/n}$.

Example   The Normal distribution $N(\mu, \sigma^2)$ is infinitely divisible. In fact:

$$\phi_N(u; \mu, \sigma) = \left(\exp\left(\frac{iu\mu}{n} \right) \exp\left(-\frac{1}{2n}\sigma^2 u^2 \right) \right)^n = (\phi_n(u))^n,$$

where $\phi_n(u)$ is the characteristic function of a Normal distribution $N(\mu/n, \sigma^2/n)$. If $Y_i^{(n)}$, $i = 1, \ldots, n$ are i.i.d. normal random variables $N(\mu/n, \sigma^2/n)$

$$X = Y_1^{(n)} + \cdots + Y_n^{(n)} \sim \text{Normal}(\mu, \sigma^2).$$

Definition 2.4 (Lévy Process)   *A stochastic process $X = \{X_t, t \geq 0\}$ is a Lévy process if the following conditions[2] hold:*

1. $X_0 = 0$.
2. *The process has stationary increments (see Definition 2.1 above).*
3. *The process has independent increments (see Definition 2.1 above).*

The law at time t of a Lévy process is completely determined by the law of X_1. The only degree of freedom we have in specifying a Lévy process is to define its distribution at a single time. If, for example, the distribution of X_1 has as characteristic function $\phi(u)$, then the distribution of an increment of $X = \{X_t, t \geq 0\}$ over $[s, s+t]$, $s, t \geq 0$, i.e. $X_{t+s} - X_s$, has $(\phi(u))^t$ as characteristic function. To be precise, the following theorem describes the one-to-one relationship between Lévy processes and infinitely divisible distributions.

Theorem 2.1 (Infinite Divisibility of Lévy Processes)   *Let $X = \{X_t, t \geq 0\}$ be a Lévy process. Then $X = \{X_t, t \geq 0\}$ has an infinitely divisible distribution F for every t. Conversely if F is an infinitely divisible distribution there exists a Lévy process $X = \{X_t, t \geq 0\}$ such that the distribution of X_1 is given by F.*

Further, we can write

$$\phi_{X_t}(u) = \mathbb{E}\left[\exp(iuX_t) \right] = \exp(t\psi(u))$$

where $\psi(u) = \log(\phi(u))$ is the characteristic exponent as in Equation (2.6).

---

[2] To be mathematically precise we have to also impose a technical condition, namely that X_t is a stochastically continuous process:

$$\forall \varepsilon > 0 \quad \lim_{h \to 0} \mathbb{P}\left(|X_{t+h} - X_t| \geq \varepsilon\right) = 0.$$

Note that this condition does not imply that the path of Lévy processes are continuous. It only requires that for a given time t, the probability of seeing a jump at t is zero, i.e. jumps occur at random times. A technical discussion on stochastic continuity and cadlag paths can be found in Sato (1999).

The characteristic exponent $\psi(u)$ of a Lévy process satisfies the following *Lévy–Khintchine formula* (Bertoin 1996):

$$\psi(u) = i\gamma u - \frac{\varsigma^2}{2}u^2 + \int_{-\infty}^{+\infty} (\exp(iux) - 1 - iux\mathbf{1}_{\{|x|<1\}})\nu(dx), \qquad (2.7)$$

where $\gamma \in \mathbb{R}$, $\varsigma^2 \geq 0$, $\mathbf{1}_A$ is the indicator function of A, and ν is a measure on $\mathbb{R}\backslash\{0\}$ such that

$$\int_{-\infty}^{+\infty} \min\{1, x^2\}\nu(dx) = \int_{-\infty}^{+\infty} (1 \wedge x^2)\nu(dx) < \infty.$$

From the Lévy–Khintchine formula, one sees that, in general, a Lévy process consists of three independent parts: a linear deterministic part, a Brownian part, and a pure jump part. We say that the corresponding infinitely divisible distribution has a Lévy triplet $[\gamma, \varsigma^2, \nu(dx)]$. From Equation (2.7) we can deduce that Brownian motion is a Lévy process. Recalling Equation (2.5), we see that the Brownian motion triplet is $[\mu, \sigma^2, 0]$.

The measure ν is called the *Lévy measure* of X and it dictates how jumps occur: jumps of sizes in the set A occur according to a Poisson process with parameter $\nu(A) = \int_A \nu(dx)$. In other words, $\nu(A)$ is the expected number of jumps per unit time, whose size belongs to A.

If $\sigma^2 = 0$ and $\int_{-1}^{+1} |x|\nu(dx) < \infty$, it follows from standard Lévy process theory (Bertoin 1996, Sato 1999, Kyprianou 2006) that the process is of finite variation. Moreover, there is a finite number of jumps in any finite interval and the process is said to be of finite activity.

Because the Brownian motion is of infinite variation, a Lévy process with a Brownian component is of infinite variation. A pure jump Lévy process, i.e. with no Brownian component ($\sigma^2 = 0$), is of infinite variation if and only if $\int_{-1}^{+1} |x|\nu(dx) = \infty$. In that case, special attention has to be paid to the small jumps. Basically the sum of all jumps smaller than some $\varepsilon > 0$ does not converge. However the sum of the jumps compensated by their mean does converge. This peculiarity leads to the necessity of the compensator term $iux\mathbf{1}_{\{|x|<1\}}$ in (2.7).

2.3 EXAMPLES OF LÉVY PROCESSES

The examples presented in this section cover only the Lévy processes used in this book. For other examples, see Appelbaum (2004), Schoutens (2003) or Kyprianou (2006).

2.3.1 Poisson Process

The Poisson process is the most simple pure jump Lévy process we can think of. It is based on the Poisson distribution, which depends on a single parameter λ and

Table 2.2 Moments of the Poisson
distribution with intensity λ

	Poisson(λ)
Mean	λ
Variance	λ
Skewness	$1/\sqrt{\lambda}$
Kurtosis	$3 + \lambda^{-1}$

has the following characteristic function:

$$\phi_{\text{Poisson}}(u; \lambda) = \exp(\lambda(\exp(iu) - 1)).$$

The Poisson distribution lives on the non-negative integers $\{0, 1, 2, \ldots\}$; the probability mass at point j equals

$$\exp(-\lambda)\lambda^j/j!.$$

The moments of the Poisson distribution are reported in Table 2.2.

Since the Poisson(λ) distribution is infinitely divisible, we can, following Theorem 2.1, define a Poisson process as follows:

Definition 2.5 (*Poisson Process*) *A stochastic process $N = \{N_t, t \geq 0\}$ with intensity parameter $\lambda > 0$ is a Poisson process if it fulfils the following conditions:*

1. $N_0 = 0$.
2. *The process has independent increments.*
3. *The process has stationary increments.*
4. *For $0s < t$ the random variable $N_t - N_s$ has a Poisson distribution with parameter $\lambda(t - s)$:*

$$P(N_t - N_s = n) = \frac{\lambda^n (t - s)^n}{n!} \exp(-\lambda (t - s)).$$

The Poisson process is an increasing pure jump process, with jump sizes always equal to 1. The Lévy triplet is given by $[0, 0, \lambda\delta(1)]$, where $\delta(1)$ denotes the Dirac measure at point 1, i.e. a measure with only mass 1 in the point 1. The time in between two consecutive jumps follows an exponential distribution with mean λ^{-1}, i.e. a Gamma$(1, \lambda)$ law (see Section 2.3.3).

This latter property can be used to simulate a Poisson process as follows:

1. Generate an uniform random number u_n.
2. Generate an Exp(λ) random number e_n by setting $e_n = -\log(u_n)/\lambda$.

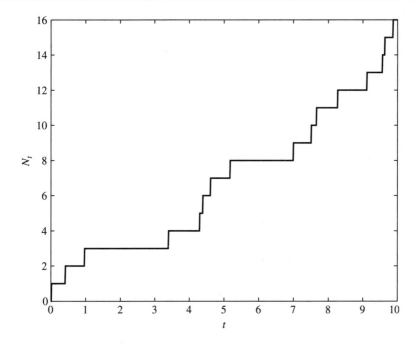

Figure 2.4   A sample path of a Poisson process with parameter $\lambda = 0.5$

3. Set $s_0 = 0, \quad s_n = s_{n-1} + e_n, \quad n = 1, 2, \ldots$.
4. A sample path of a Poisson with intensity λ, in the time points $\{n\Delta t, n = 0, 1, \ldots\}$ is given by:

$$N_0 = 0, \quad N_{n\Delta t} = \sup (k : s_k \leq n\Delta t).$$

Figure 2.4 shows a typical Poisson path, with intensity parameter $\lambda = 0.5$.

2.3.2   Compound Poisson Process

Definition 2.6 (*Compound Poisson Process*)   *A compound Poisson process with intensity λ and jumps size distribution L is a stochastic process $X = \{X_t, t \geq 0\}$ defined as*

$$X_t = \sum_{k=1}^{N_t} Z_k, \quad t \geq 0,$$

where jumps size Z_k are i.i.d. with law L and $N = \{N_t, t \geq 0\}$ is a Poisson process with intensity parameter λ, independent of $(Z_k, k = 1, 2, \ldots)$.

The sample paths of $X = \{X_t, t \geq 0\}$ are piecewise constant and the value of the process at time t, X_t, is the sum of N_t random numbers with law L. The jump times have the same law as those of the Poisson process $N = \{N_t, t \geq 0\}$. The ordinary Poisson process corresponds to the case where $Z_k = 1$, $k = 1, 2, \ldots$, i.e. where the law L is degenerate in the point 1.

Let us define (for a Borel set A) the measure ν as follows:

$$\nu(A) = \lambda \mathbb{P}(Z_i \in A).$$

Note that $\nu(\mathbb{R}) = \lambda < \infty$. We impose that $\nu(\{0\}) = 0$. Then it can be shown that the characteristic function of $X = \{X_t, t \geq 0\}$ is given by

$$\mathbb{E}[\exp(iuX_t)] = \exp\left(t \int_{-\infty}^{+\infty} (\exp(iux) - 1)\nu(dx) \right)$$
$$= \exp\left(t\lambda(\phi_Z(u) - 1) \right),$$

where $\phi_Z(u)$ is the characteristic function of the law L. From this we can easily obtain the Lévy triplet $[\int_{-1}^{+1} x\nu(dx), 0, \nu(dx)]$. Figure 2.5 shows a compound Poisson process with intensity $\lambda = 0.5$, jump sizes distributed as a Standard Normal, and corresponding to the intensity process $N = \{N_t, t \geq 0\}$ presented in Figure 2.4.

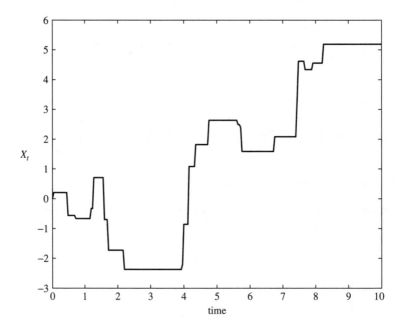

Figure 2.5 A sample path of a compound Poisson process with parameter $\lambda = 0.5$ and jumps sizes distributed as a Standard Normal

2.3.3 The Gamma Process

The Gamma distribution is characterized by two positive parameters, $a > 0$ and $b > 0$. The density function of a Gamma(a, b) distribution is given by

$$f_{\text{Gamma}}(x; a, b) = \frac{b^a}{\Gamma(a)} x^{a-1} \exp(-xb), \quad x > 0. \tag{2.8}$$

The moments of the Gamma(a, b) distribution are reported in Table 2.3. Figure 2.6 shows the dependence of the Gamma(a, b) distribution on the 'shape' parameter b. Moreover, the following scaling property holds: if X is a Gamma(a, b) random variable, then for $c > 0$, cX is a Gamma$(a, b/c)$ random variable.

Table 2.3 Moments of the Gamma(a, b) distribution

	Gamma(a, b)
Mean	a/b
Variance	a/b^2
Skewness	$2a^{-1/2}$
Kurtosis	$3(1 + 2a^{-1})$

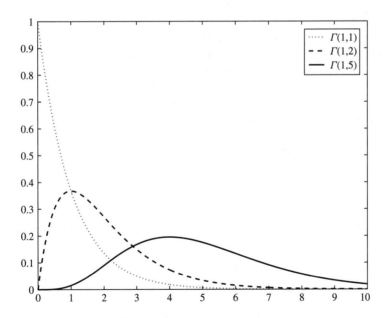

Figure 2.6 Gamma distributions for various sets of parameters (a, b)

The density function clearly has a semi-heavy (right) tail.[3] The characteristic function is given by

$$\phi_{\text{Gamma}}(u; a, b) = (1 - iu/b)^{-a}.$$

This characteristic function is infinitely divisible. On the virtue of Theorem 2.1 one can thus define a Gamma process as follows:

Definition 2.7 (*Gamma Process*)   *A stochastic process* $X^{\text{Gamma}} = \{X_t^{\text{Gamma}}, t \geq 0\}$ *with parameters a and b is a Gamma process if it fulfils the following conditions:*

1. $X_0^{\text{Gamma}} = 0$.
2. *The process has independent increments.*
3. *The process has stationary increments.*
4. *For 0s < t the random variable* $X_t^{\text{Gamma}} - X_s^{\text{Gamma}}$ *has a Gamma*$(a(t-s), b)$ *distribution.*

The Gamma process is a non-decreasing Lévy process and one can show, after some tedious calculations, that its Lévy triplet is given by

$$[a(1 - \exp(-b))/b, 0, a \exp(-bx)x^{-1}1_{(x>0)} \, dx].$$

A Gamma process with parameters a and b can be simulated in the time points $\{n\Delta t, n = 0, 1, \ldots\}$ as:

$$X_0^{\text{Gamma}} = 0, \quad X_{n\Delta t}^{\text{Gamma}} = X_{(n-1)\Delta t}^{\text{Gamma}} + g_n,$$

where $\{g_n, n \geq 1\}$ is a sequence of Gamma$(a\Delta t, b)$ random variables. Gamma random variable generators are available in the most common statistical software packages, or one can, for instance, refer to Devroye (1986). Figure 2.7 shows a path for a Gamma process with parameters $a = 0.5$ and $b = 2$.

Later on we will sometimes make use of stochastic processes built out of a Gamma-process $X^{\text{Gamma}} = \{X_t^{\text{Gamma}}, t \geq 0\}$ with parameters $a > 0$ and $b > 0$. A Shifted Gamma (SG) process, for example, is obtained by subtracting the Gamma process from a deterministic trend:

$$X_t^{\text{SG}} = \mu t - X_t^{\text{Gamma}}, \quad t \geq 0.$$

---

[3] We say that a distribution or its density function $f(x)$ has semi-heavy tails, if the tails of the density function behave as

$$f(x) \sim C_-|x|^{\rho_-} \exp(-\eta_-|x|) \quad \text{as} \quad x \to -\infty$$

$$f(x) \sim C_+|x|^{\rho_+} \exp(-\eta_+|x|) \quad \text{as} \quad x \to +\infty,$$

for some $\rho_-, \rho_+ \in \mathbb{R}$ and $C_-, C_+, \eta_-, \eta_+ \geq 0$. The Normal distribution does not belong to this class, since $\log(f(x))$ is quadratic in x. The Normal distribution is therefore said to have light-tail behaviour.

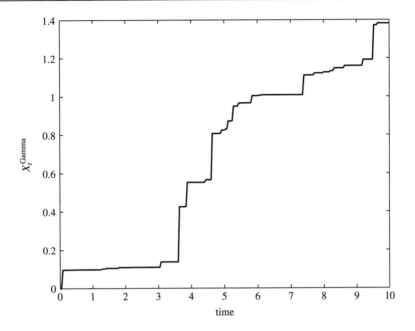

Figure 2.7 Simulated Gamma process with parameters $a = 0.5$ and $b = 2$

2.3.4 Inverse Gaussian Process

Let $T^{(a,b)}$ be the first time standard Brownian motion with drift $b > 0$, i.e. $\{W_s + bs, s \geq 0\}$ reaches the positive level $a > 0$. This random time follows the so-called Inverse Gaussian law, IG(a, b), and has as characteristic function

$$\phi_{IG}(u; a, b) = \exp\left(-a(\sqrt{-2iu + b^2} - b)\right). \tag{2.**}$$

The density function of the IG(a, b) law is explicitly known:

$$f_{IG}(x; a, b) = \frac{a}{\sqrt{2\pi}} \exp(ab) x^{-3/2} \exp(-(a^2 x^{-1} + b^2 x)/2), \quad x > 0. \tag{2.9}$$

Table 2.4 describes the characteristics of the IG distribution. Moreover, the IG distribution satisfies the following scaling property: if X is IG(a, b), for any positive c, cX is IG$(\sqrt{c}a, b/\sqrt{c})$.

The IG distribution is infinitely divisible and we can thus define the IG process $X^{(IG)} = \{X_t^{(IG)}, t \geq 0\}$, with parameters $a, b > 0$ as the process which starts at zero, has independent and stationary increments, and is such that its characteristic function is given by:

$$\mathbb{E}[\exp(iu X_t^{(IG)})] = \phi_{IG}(u; at, b) = \exp\left(-at(\sqrt{-2iu + b^2} - b)\right).$$

Table 2.4 Moments of the
IG(a, b) distribution

	IG(a, b)
Mean	a/b
Variance	a/b^3
Skewness	$3(ab)^{-1/2}$
Kurtosis	$3(1 + 5(ab)^{-1})$

The Lévy measure of the IG(a, b) is given by:

$$\nu_{\text{IG}}(\mathrm{d}x) = (2\pi)^{-1/2}ax^{-3/2}\exp(-b^2x/2)1_{(x>0)}\,\mathrm{d}x$$

and the first component of the Lévy triplet equals

$$\gamma = \frac{a}{b}(2\Phi(b) - 1),$$

where Φ is the Standard Normal distribution function as in (2.1). Note that the IG process is a non-decreasing Lévy process.

To simulate an IG process with parameters a and b in the time points $\{n\Delta t, n = 0, 1, \ldots\}$, we can use the following typical scheme:

$$X_0^{\text{IG}} = 0, \quad X_{n\Delta t}^{\text{IG}} = X_{(n-1)\Delta t}^{\text{IG}} + i_n$$

where $\{i_n, n \geq 1\}$ is a sequence of IG($a\Delta t, b$) random variables. To simulate an IG(a, b) random variable we follow the algorithm proposed by Michael *et al.* (1976):

1. Generate a normal random variable ν,
2. Set $y = \nu^2$,
3. Set $x = a/b + y/(2b^2) - \sqrt{4aby + y^2}/(2b^2)$,
4. Generate a uniform random variable u,
5. If $u \leq a/(a + xb)$, then return the number x as the IG(a, b) random number; otherwise return $a^2/(b^2x)$ as the IG(a, b) random number.

Figure 2.8 shows a path for an Inverse Gaussian process with parameters $a = 0.2$ and $b = 1$.

As in the Gamma case, here we will sometimes work with processes built out of the IG process $X^{\text{IG}} = \{X_t^{\text{IG}}, t \geq 0\}$. A Shifted IG (SIG) process is for example

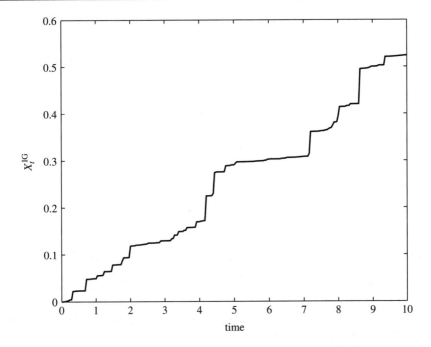

Figure 2.8 Simulated Gamma process with parameters $a = 0.2$ and $b = 0.1$

obtained by subtracting X^{IG} from a deterministic trend:

$$X_t^{\text{SIG}} = \mu t - X_t^{\text{IG}}, \quad t \geq 0.$$

2.3.5 The CMY Process

The characteristic function of the CMY distribution $\text{CMY}(C, M, Y)$ with parameters $C, M > 0$ and $Y < 1$ is given by:

$$\phi_{\text{CMY}}(u; C, M, Y) = \exp(C\Gamma(-Y)((M - iu)^Y - M^Y)).$$

Note that the CMY distribution is sometimes also referred to (with another parameter convention) as a Tempered Stable distribution.

The Lévy measure of the CMY process is given by:

$$\nu_{\text{CMY}}(x) = C \exp(-Mx)x^{-1-Y}\,\mathrm{d}x, \qquad x > 0. \tag{2.10}$$

Table 2.5   Mean, variance, skewness and kurtosis of the CMY(C, M, Y) distribution

	CMY(C, M, Y)
Mean	$CM^{Y-1}\Gamma(1-Y)$
Variance	$CM^{Y-2}\Gamma(2-Y)$
Skewness	$\dfrac{CM^{Y-3}\Gamma(3-Y)}{(CM^{Y-2}\Gamma(2-Y))^{3/2}}$
Kurtosis	$3 + \dfrac{CM^{Y-4}\Gamma(4-Y)}{(CM^{Y-2}\Gamma(2-Y))^{2}}$

Observe from the Gamma and IG Lévy densities that the corresponding Lévy processes are special cases of the CMY process; take $Y = 0$ and $Y = 1/2$ respectively.

Clearly the characteristic function (2.**) is infinitely divisible. The CMY process $C = \{C_t, t \geq 0\}$ with parameters $C, M > 0$ and $Y < 1$ is defined as the stochastic process which starts at zero and has stationary, independent CMY-distributed increments. More precisely, the time enters in the first parameter: C_t follows a CMY(Ct, M, Y) distribution.

The properties of the CMY(C, M, Y) distribution given in Table 2.5 can easily be derived from the characteristic function.

A process related to the CMY process is the Shifted CMY. Let us start with a CMY process $C = \{C_t, t \geq 0\}$ with parameters $C, M > 0$ and $Y < 1$. The Shifted CMY (SCMY) is then defined as

$$X_t = \mu t - C_t, \quad t \geq 0.$$

We hence have a deterministic up-trend and negative jumps from a CMY process.

2.3.6   The Variance Gamma Process

The Variance Gamma (VG) distribution is characterized by a triplet of positive parameters (C, G, M). It is defined on $(-\infty, +\infty)$ and its density function is given by

$$f_{VG}(z; C, G, M) = \frac{(GM)^C}{\sqrt{\pi}\,\Gamma(C)} \exp\left(\frac{(G-M)z}{2}\right)$$

$$\times \left(\frac{|z|}{G+M}\right)^{C-1/2} K_{C-1/2}\big((G+M)\,|z|/2\big),$$

where $K_\nu(z)$ denotes the modified Bessel function of the third kind with index ν and $\Gamma(z)$ denotes the gamma function.

A VG random variable can be constructed as the difference of two gamma random variables. Suppose that X is a Gamma($a = C, b = M$) random variable and that Y is a Gamma($a = C, b = G$) random variable and that they are independent of each other. Then

$$Z = X - Y \sim \text{VG}(C, G, M).$$

To derive the characteristic function of the VG(C, G, M) distribution, we start with noting that

$$\phi_X(u) = (1 - iu/M)^{-C} \quad \text{and} \quad \phi_Y(u) = (1 - iu/G)^{-C}.$$

By using the property of the characteristic function $\phi_{-X}(u) = \phi_X(-u)$, we have

$$\phi_{-Y}(u) = (1 + iu/G)^{-C}.$$

Summing the two independent random variables X and $-Y$ and using the convolution property (2.4) gives

$$\phi_Z(u; C, G, M) = \phi_{X-Y}(u) = (1 - iu/M)^{-C}(1 + iu/G)^{-C}$$

$$= \left(\frac{GM}{GM + (M - G)iu + u^2} \right)^C. \tag{2.11}$$

Another way of introducing the VG distribution is by mixing a Normal distribution with a Gamma random variate:

1. Take a random variate $X \sim \text{Gamma}(a = 1/\nu, b = 1/\nu)$.
2. Sample a random variate $Z \sim \text{Normal}(\theta X, \sigma^2 X)$. Then Z follows a VG distribution.

The distribution of Z is denoted in this case by VG(σ, ν, θ). The parameters ν and σ are positive, while $\theta \in (-\infty, \infty)$.

One can show, using basic probabilistic techniques, that under this parameter setting the characteristic function of the VG(σ, ν, θ) law is given by

$$\phi_{\text{VG}}(u; \sigma, \nu, \theta) = \mathbb{E}[\exp(iuZ)] = (1 - iu\theta\nu + \sigma^2\nu u^2/2)^{-1/\nu}. \tag{2.12}$$

The relation between the two parameterizations (C, G, M) and (σ, ν, θ) is given by:

$$C = 1/\nu > 0$$

Table 2.6 Moments of the VG distribution under the two parameterizations

	VG(C, G, M)	VG(σ, v, θ)
Mean	$C(G - M)/(MG)$	θ
Variance	$C(G^2 + M^2)/(MG)^2$	$\sigma^2 + v\theta^2$
Skewness	$2C^{-1/2}(G^3 - M^3)/(G^2 + M^2)^{3/2}$	$\theta v(3\sigma^2 + 2v\theta^2)/(\sigma^2 + v\theta^2)^{3/2}$
Kurtosis	$3(1 + 2C^{-1}(G^4 + M^4)/(M^2 + G^2)^2)$	$3(1 + 2v - v\sigma^4(\sigma^2 + v\theta^2)^{-2})$

$$G = \left(\sqrt{\frac{\theta^2 v^2}{4} + \frac{\sigma^2 v}{2}} - \frac{\theta v}{2} \right)^{-1} > 0$$

$$M = \left(\sqrt{\frac{\theta^2 v^2}{4} + \frac{\sigma^2 v}{2}} + \frac{\theta v}{2} \right)^{-1} > 0.$$

Vice versa we have:

$$v = 1/C$$
$$\sigma^2 = 2C/(MG)$$
$$\theta = C(G - M)/(MG).$$

Table 2.6 describes the moments of the VG distribution in terms of the two parameterizations. As shown in Figure 2.9, the VG distribution is very flexible. The top plot of Figure 2.9 shows the sensitivity of the VG distribution to the θ parameter. When $\theta = 0$ the distribution is symmetric. Negative values of θ result in negative skewness; positive θ's give positive skewness. The parameter v (bottom plot of Figure 2.9) primarily controls the kurtosis. In terms of the (C, G, M) parameters $G = M$ give the symmetric case, $G < M$ results in negative skewness and $G > M$ gives rise to positive skewness. The parameter C controls the kurtosis.

The class of VG distributions was introduced by Madan and Seneta (1987) in the late 1980s as a model for stock returns. There (and in Madan and Seneta 1990 and Madan and Milne 1991) the symmetric case ($\theta = 0$) was considered. In Madan *et al.* (1998), the general case with skewness is treated. For some background on the early years of the VG process, see Seneta (2007).

The VG distribution is infinitely divisible and thus one can define the VG process.

Definition 2.8 (VG Process) *A stochastic process $X^{\text{VG}} = \{X_t^{\text{VG}}, t \geq 0\}$ is a VG process if it fulfils the following properties:*

1. $X_0^{\text{VG}} = 0$.
2. *The process has independent increments.*
3. *The process has stationary increments.*

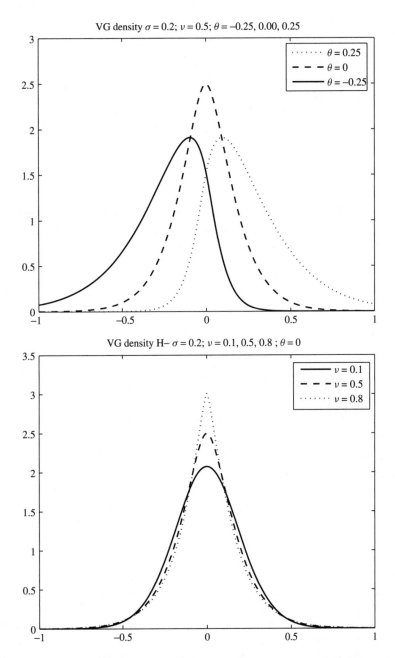

Figure 2.9 Sensitivity of the VG distribution to the parameter θ (top plot) and ν (bottom plot)

4. *The increment $X^{VG}_{s+t} - X^{VG}_s$ over the time interval $[s, t+s]$ follows a* VG$(\sigma \sqrt{t}, v/t, t\theta)$ *law given by Equation (2.12).*

Under the (C, G, M) parameterization, the third condition can be rephrased as the increment $X^{VG}_{s+t} - X^{VG}_s$ over the time interval $[s, s+t]$ follows a VG(Ct, G, M) law given by Equation (2.11).

In line with the property of the VG(C, G, M) distribution, a VG process can be expressed as the difference of two independent Gamma processes (Madan *et al.* 1998) as follows:

$$X^{VG}_t = G^{(1)}_t - G^{(2)}_t,$$

where $G^{(1)} = \{G^{(1)}_t, t \geq 0\}$ is a Gamma process with parameters $a = C$ and $b = M$ and $G^{(2)} = \{G^{(2)}_t, t \geq 0\}$ is a Gamma process with parameters $a = C$ and $b = G$. This characterization allows the Lévy measure to be determined:

$$\nu_{VG}(dx) = \begin{cases} C \exp(Gx)|x|^{-1} \, dx & x < 0 \\ C \exp(-Mx)x^{-1} \, dx & x > 0 \end{cases}. \tag{2.13}$$

The Lévy measure has infinite mass, and hence a VG process has infinitely many jumps in any finite time interval. However, since $\int_{-\infty}^{+\infty} |x| \nu_{VG}(dx) < \infty$, a VG-process has paths of finite variation. A VG process has no Brownian component and its Lévy triplet is given by $[\gamma, 0, \nu_{VG}(dx)]$, where

$$\gamma = \frac{-C(G(\exp(-M) - 1) - M(\exp(-G) - 1))}{MG}.$$

Another option is to define a VG(σ, v, θ) process as a Gamma time-changed Brownian motion with drift:

$$X^{VG}_t = \theta X^{Gamma}_t + \sigma W_{X^{Gamma}_t}$$

where $X^{Gamma} = \{X^{Gamma}_t, t \geq 0\}$ is a Gamma$(1/v, 1/v)$ process and $W = \{W_t, t \geq 0\}$ is a standard Brownian motion.

Applications of stochastic time change to asset pricing go back to Mandelbrot and Taylor (1967) (see also Clark 1973). Time change corresponds to introducing a new business time in which the general market operates. This new business time can also be interpreted as a model for the arrival of information. Taking into account that the market will not forget information, the amount of information cannot decrease. Moreover, it seems reasonable that the amount of new information released should not be affected by the amount already released, in other words, the information process should have independent increments. Finally, one can also require that the increment only depends on the length of that period and hence is

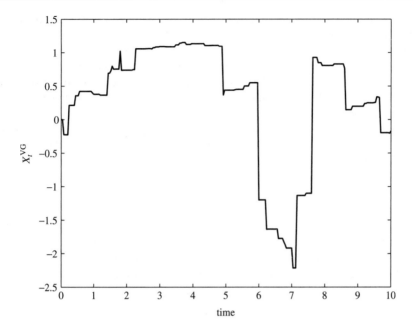

Figure 2.10   A sample path of a VG process

stationary. This leads to modelling the information process by a non-decreasing process with stationary and independent increments.

Note that in this perspective one can read the variance of Table 2.6 as the sum of an idiosyncratic component (σ^2), coming from the Brownian motion, and an exogenous component ($\nu\theta^2$) arising from the time change. When using the VG process for financial application, e.g. for modelling the behaviour of an asset, this decomposition allows for very intuitive interpretations. Note also that skewness and kurtosis are affected by the asset's own specific settings (θ and σ) as well as by the global parameter ν. Figure 2.10 shows a path of a VG process with parameters $\sigma = 0.5$, $\nu = 1.5$ and $\theta = 0.2$.

2.4   ORNSTEIN–UHLENBECK PROCESSES

Ornstein–Uhlenbeck (OU) processes (driven by Lévy processes) were introduced by Barndorff-Nielsen and Shephard (2001a, 2001b, 2003) to describe volatility in finance. Further references on the OU processes are Wolfe (1982), Sato and Yamazato (1982), Sato *et al.* (1994).

An OU process $y = \{y_t, t \geq 0\}$ is described by the following stochastic differential equation:

$$\mathrm{d}y_t = -\vartheta y_t\, \mathrm{d}t + \mathrm{d}z_{\vartheta t}, \quad y_0 > 0, \tag{2.14}$$

where ϑ is the arbitrary positive rate parameter and z_t is a non-decreasing Lévy process (often called the Background Driving Lévy Process (BDLP)).[4] As z is an increasing process and $y_0 > 0$, it is clear that the process y is strictly positive. Moreover, it is bounded from below by the deterministic function $y_0 \exp(-\vartheta t)$.

The process $y = \{y_t, t \geq 0\}$ is strictly stationary on the positive half-line, i.e. there exists a law D, called the stationary law or the marginal law, such that y_t will follow the law D for every t, if the initial y_0 is chosen according to D. The process y moves up entirely by jumps and then tails off exponentially. The fact that we have the parameter ϑ in $z_{\vartheta t}$ has to do with the separation of the stationary law from this decay parameter. In Barndorff-Nielsen and Shephard (2001a) some stochastic properties of y are studied. Barndorff-Nielsen and Shephard established the notation that if y is an OU process with marginal law D, then we say that y is a D-OU process.

In essence, given a one-dimensional distribution D (not necessarily restricted to the positive half-line) there exists a (stationary) OU process whose marginal law is D (i.e. a D-OU process) if and only if D is self-decomposable.[5] We have by standard results (Barndorff-Nielsen and Shephard 2001a) that

$$y_t = \exp(-\vartheta t) y_0 + \int_0^t \exp(-\vartheta(t-s)) \, dz_{\vartheta s}$$

$$= \exp(-\vartheta t) y_0 + \exp(-\vartheta t) \int_0^{\vartheta t} \exp(s) \, dz_s.$$

In the case of a D-OU process, let us denote by $k_D(u)$ the cumulant function of the self-decomposable law D and by $k_z(u)$ the cumulant function of the BDLP at time $t = 1$, i.e. $k_z(u) = \log \mathbb{E}[\exp(-uz_1)]$, then both are related through the formula (see, for example, Barndorff-Nielsen 2001):

$$k_z(u) = u \frac{dk_D(u)}{du}.$$

An important related process will be the integral of y. Barndorff-Nielsen and Shephard called this the integrated OU process (intOU), and we will denote this process by $Y = \{Y_t, t \geq 0\}$:

$$Y_t = \int_0^t y_s \, ds. \tag{2.15}$$

---

[4] Also OU processes based on a general Lévy process, not necessarily a non-decreasing Lévy process, can be defined. However, for our analysis we will only need the special case considered above.

[5] Let ϕ be the characteristic function of a random variable X. Then X is self-decomposable if

$$\phi(u) = \phi(cu)\phi_c(u),$$

for all $u \in \mathbb{R}$ and all $c \in [0, 1]$ and for some family of characteristic functions $\{\phi_c : c \in (0, 1)\}$. For more details see Sato (1999).

A major feature of the intOU process Y is

$$Y_t = \vartheta^{-1}(z_{\vartheta t} - y_t + y_0)$$

$$= \vartheta^{-1}(1 - \exp(-\vartheta t))y_0 + \vartheta^{-1}\int_0^t (1 - \exp(-\vartheta(t-s)))\,dz_{\vartheta s}. \quad (2.16)$$

One can show (see Barndorff-Nielsen and Shephard 2001a) that, given y_0,

$$\log \mathbb{E}[\exp(iuY_t)|y_0] = \vartheta \int_0^t k(u\vartheta^{-1}(1 - \exp(-\vartheta(t-s))))\,ds$$

$$+ iuy_0\vartheta^{-1}(1 - \exp(-\vartheta t)),$$

where $k(u) = k_z(u) = \log \mathbb{E}[\exp(-uz_1)]$ is the cumulant function of z_1.

2.4.1 The Gamma-OU Process

The Gamma(a, b)-OU process has as Background Driving Lévy Process (BDLP), a compound Poisson process (see Section 2.3.2):

$$z_t = \sum_{n=1}^{N_t} x_n$$

where $N = \{N_t, t \geq 0\}$ is a Poisson process with intensity $a\vartheta$ (i.e. $\mathbb{E}[N_t] = at$) and $\{x_n, n = 1, 2, \ldots\}$ is a sequence of independent identically distributed Exp(b) variables, i.e. exponentially distributed with mean $1/b$. It turns out that the stationary law is given by a Gamma(a, b) distribution of Equation (2.8), which immediately explains the name. The Gamma-OU process has a finite number of jumps in every compact time interval.

If y_t is a Gamma-OU process, the characteristic function of the intOU process $Y_t = \int_0^t y_s\,ds$ is given by:

$$\phi_{\text{Gamma-OU}}(u, t; \vartheta, a, b, y_0) = \mathbb{E}[\exp(iuY_t)|y_0]$$

$$= \exp\left(\frac{iuy_0}{\vartheta}(1 - e^{-\vartheta t}) + \frac{\vartheta a}{iu - \vartheta b}\right.$$

$$\left.\times \left(b\log\left(\frac{b}{b - iu\vartheta^{-1}(1 - e^{-\vartheta t})}\right) - iut\right)\right).$$

$$(2.17)$$

A Gamma(a, b)-OU process $\{y_t, t \geq 0\}$ can be simulated at time points $\{t = n\Delta t, n = 0, 1, 2, \ldots\}$ throughout its BDLP as follows:

1. Simulate, at the same time points $\{t = n\Delta t, n = 0, 1, 2, \ldots\}$ a Poisson process $\{N_t, t \geq 0\}$ with intensity parameter $a\vartheta$,
2. Generate $\{x_n, n = 0, 1, \ldots\}$ (independent) Exp(b) random numbers;

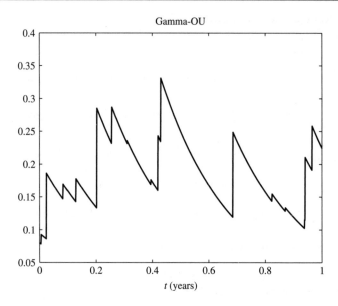

Figure 2.11 Gamma-OU simulated sample path

3. Generate $\{u_n, n = 0, 1, \ldots\}$ (independent) standard uniform random numbers.
4. Set:

$$y_{n\Delta t} = \exp(-\vartheta \,\Delta t) y_{(n-1)\Delta t} + \sum_{n=N_{(n-1)\Delta t}+1}^{N_{n\Delta t}} x_n \exp(-u_n \vartheta \,\Delta t). \qquad (2.18)$$

Note that the exponential term and the uniform random numbers u_n in the sum allows the jumps to happen somewhere in between two time steps. Figure 2.11 shows a path of a Gamma-OU process with parameters $\vartheta = 4$, $a = 4$, $b = 18$ and $y_0 = 0.08$.

2.4.2 The Inverse Gaussian-OU Process

The IG-OU process is based on the IG(a, b) distribution given in Equation (2.9). This distribution belongs to the class of the self-decomposable distributions and hence an IG-OU process exists. In the case of the IG(a, b)-OU process the BDLP is a sum of two independent Lévy processes $z = \{z_t = z_t^{(1)} + z_t^{(2)}, t \geq 0\}$. $z^{(1)}$ is an IG-Lévy process with parameters $a/2$ and b, while $z^{(2)}$ is of the form:

$$z_t^{(2)} = b^{-1} \sum_{n=1}^{N_t} v_n^2,$$

where $N = \{N_t, t \geq 0\}$ is a Poisson process with intensity parameter $ab/2$, i.e. $\mathbb{E}[N_t] = abt/2$. $\{v_n, n = 1, 2, \ldots\}$ is a sequence of iid random variables: each v_n

follows a Normal(0, 1) law independent from the Poisson process N. Since the BDLP (via $z^{(1)}$) jumps infinitely often in any finite (time) interval, the IG-OU process also jumps infinitely often in every interval. The cumulant of the BDLP (at time 1) is given by

$$k(u) = -uab^{-1}(1 + 2ub^{-2})^{-1/2}.$$

In the IG-OU case the characteristic function of the intOU process $Y_t = \int_0^t y_s \, ds$ can also be given explicitly. The following expression was independently derived in Nicolato and Venardos (2003) and Tompkins and Hubalek (2000):

$$\phi_{\text{IG-OU}}(u, t; \vartheta, a, b, y_0) = \mathbb{E}[\exp(iuY_t)|y_0]$$

$$= \exp\left(\frac{iuy_0}{\vartheta}(1 - \exp^{(-\vartheta t)}) + \frac{2aiu}{b\vartheta}A(u, t)\right), \quad (2.19)$$

where

$$A(u, t) = \frac{1 - \sqrt{1 + \kappa(1 - \exp(-\vartheta t))}}{\kappa} + \frac{1}{\sqrt{1 + \kappa}}$$

$$\times \left[\text{arctanh}\left(\frac{\sqrt{1 + \kappa(1 - \exp(-\vartheta t))}}{\sqrt{1 + \kappa}}\right) - \text{arctanh}\left(\frac{1}{\sqrt{1 + \kappa}}\right)\right],$$

$$(2.20)$$

$$\kappa = -2b^{-2}iu/\vartheta.$$

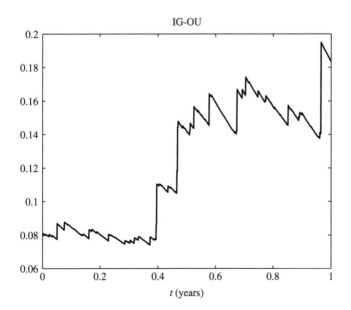

Figure 2.12 Inverse Gaussian-OU simulated sample path

The IG-OU process can be simulated by first simulating its BDLP and then applying the Euler's scheme to Equation (2.14). Fast simulation of the BDLP is achieved by recalling that the BDLP is the sum of two independent Lévy processes. Figure 2.12 shows a path of an IG-OU process with parameters $\vartheta = 2$, $a = 1.5$, $b = 12$ and $y_0 = 0.08$.

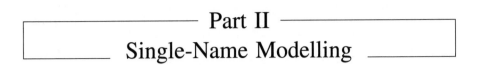

Part II
Single-Name Modelling

3
Single-Name Credit Derivatives

3.1 CREDIT DEFAULT SWAPS

Credit Default Swaps (CDSs) are the simplest and most popular credit derivatives. A CDS is a bilateral agreement where the protection buyer transfers the credit risk of a reference entity to the protection seller for a determined amount of time T. The buyer of this protection makes predetermined payments to the seller. The payments continue until the maturity date T of the contract, or until default occurs, whichever is earlier. In the case of default of the reference entity, the contract provides that the protection buyer pays to the protection seller a determined amount. Figure 3.1 presents schematically the building blocks of a CDS contract.

The *CDS spread* is the yearly rate paid by the protection buyer to enter a CDS contract against the default of the reference entity, reflecting the riskiness of the underlying credit.

Besides being used as insurance-type products, CDSs are also traded on the market for speculative purposes. Indeed, as demonstrated by Table 1.1 in Section 1.3, the market for CDSs is well established and trading is also increasing in related products like forwards and options on these CDSs.

To understand the essence of a CDS, let us consider the simple case where a person owns a defaultable bond of a company with face value $N = 10,000$ euros and maturity $T = 3$ years. Suppose this person wants to cover himself against default of this bond, i.e. the defaultable bond is our reference entity. To cover

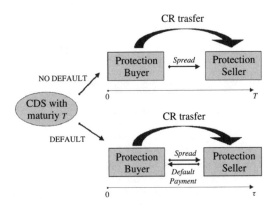

Figure 3.1   Building block of a CDS

himself, this person can enter a CDS contract of the same maturity as the defaultable bond. Thus, he becomes the protection buyer. Suppose the CDS contract states that the protection buyer needs to pay a yearly rate of 400 bps to be protected against the default of this bond. Suppose, further, that payments are made quarterly. Hence he will pay quarterly an amount of 400/4 = 100 bps on 10,000 euros, which is 100 euros, i.e. 400 euros is the yearly cost of the risk the protection seller is taking. Let us have a look at two different scenarios that can happen:

- The bond does not default before maturity. In this case the protection buyer has paid each year 400 euros to the protection seller. Note that at maturity he receives the face value of $N = 10,000$ euros via his bond position.
- The bond defaults at the beginning of the 8th quarter. Thus, the protection buyer has already paid for seven quarters at 100 euros per quarter. Due to the default, the protection seller has to settle the protection buyer with the difference between N and the recovery value after default. Suppose the recovery rate is $R = 40\%$ for our protection buyer (i.e. the recovery value is 4,000 euros). The protection seller will pay an amount equal to $N(1 - R) = 6,000$ euros. After default no further fee is paid by the protection buyer to the protection seller. The cash flows for this second scenario are presented in Figure 3.2.

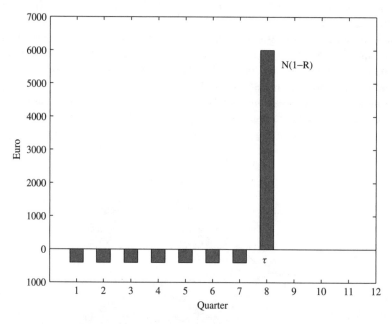

Figure 3.2 Protection buyer cash flow for a CDS with maturity $T = 3$ years, in case a default occurs at time $\tau = 2$ years. The reference entity is assumed to be a defaultable bond with face value $N = 10,000$ euros at maturity and a recovery value of 4,000 euros (i.e. the recovery rate is $R = 40\%$). We have quarterly payments. The CDS spread is 400 bps per annum

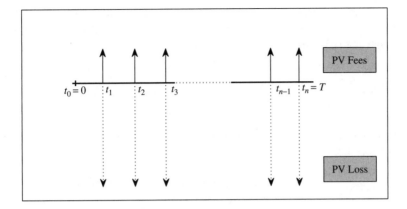

Figure 3.3 CDS pricing in discrete times

3.1.1 Credit Default Swaps Pricing

In order to understand how to price a CDS with maturity T, let us denote by c the spread of the contract per annum. Let the notional amount be N. Payments occur at discrete times t_i, $i = 1, 2, \ldots, n$ with $t_n = T$, as shown in Figure 3.3. We thus consider a discrete-time setting, e.g. think of quarterly payments. For convenience, we set $t_0 = 0$.

We assume, for the sake of simplicity, that fee and loss payments are made at the end of each period; the first time at t_1 and the last time at maturity (in case of no default).

If $D(0, t_i)$ is the discounting factor for time t_i and Δt_i the time difference between two consecutive payments ($\Delta t_i = t_i - t_{i-1}$), the present value of the fee leg (PV Fees in Figure 3.3) paid by the protection buyer is:

$$\mathrm{PV}_{\mathrm{Fees}}^{T-\mathrm{CDS}} = cN \sum_{i=1}^{n} D(0, t_i) P_{\mathrm{Surv}}(t_i) \Delta t_i, \tag{3.1}$$

where $P_{\mathrm{Surv}}(t_i)$ indicates the survival probability up to time t_i and c the par spread per annum. Equation (3.1) can be rewritten as:

$$\mathrm{PV}_{\mathrm{Fees}}^{T-\mathrm{CDS}} = cN \times A(0, T)$$

where $A(0, T)$ is the so-called *CDS risk annuity*, i.e. the present value of the premium leg of a CDS with maturity T assuming a premium of 1 bp and a unit notional amount:

$$A(0, T) = \sum_{i=1}^{n} D(0, t_i) P_{\mathrm{Surv}}(t_i) \Delta t_i. \tag{3.2}$$

Concerning the amount paid by the protection seller in case of default of the reference entity (where R denotes the recovery rate), we have that the present value of the loss leg (PV Loss in Figure 3.3) is

$$\text{PV}_{\text{Loss}}^{T-\text{CDS}} = (1 - R)N \sum_{i=1}^{n} D(0, t_i)(P_{\text{Surv}}(t_{i-1}) - P_{\text{Surv}}(t_i)). \tag{3.3}$$

Pricing the CDS is equivalent to finding the par spread $c^{T-\text{CDS}}$, which makes the premium leg equal to the loss leg:

$$c^{T-\text{CDS}} = \frac{(1 - R) \sum_{i=1}^{n} D(0, t_i)(P_{\text{Surv}}(t_{i-1}) - P_{\text{Surv}}(t_i))}{\sum_{i=1}^{n} D(0, t_i) P_{\text{Surv}}(t_i) \Delta t_i}. \tag{3.4}$$

Moving to continuous time, the constant yearly continuous par spread is obtained as:

$$c^{T-\text{CDS}} = \frac{(1 - R) \left(- \int_0^T D(0, s) \, dP_{\text{Surv}}(s) \right)}{\int_0^T D(0, s) P_{\text{Surv}}(s) \, ds}. \tag{3.5}$$

Often an accrual on default is also included. This is done to take into account the fact that if default occurs between some payment dates, fee has to be paid only for the portion between the last payment date and the time of default since the insurance buyer has been protected only for that period. An approximation to have the accrual factored into the fee leg is to assume that on average defaults happen right in the middle of a payment period and hence

$$\text{PV}_{\text{Fees}}^{T-\text{CDS}} = cN \sum_{i=1}^{n} D(0, t_i) P_{\text{Surv}}(t_i) \Delta t_i + A_D, \tag{3.6}$$

where and A_D is the accrual on default

$$A_D = c \frac{1}{2} N \sum_{i=1}^{n} D(0, t_i)(P_{\text{Surv}}(t_{i-1}) - P_{\text{Surv}}(t_i)) \Delta t_i.$$

and the fair spread formulas are changed accordingly.

Example   Given the recovery rate and the discount factor, it is clear that the CDS spread is a function of the survival probability. For instance, if we hypothesize that the default time τ is exponentially distributed with parameter λ (i.e. $\mathbb{E}[\tau] = 1/\lambda$), the survival probability is given by:

$$P_{\text{Surv}}(t) = \exp(-\lambda t),$$

and, by Equation (3.5), we obtain that the par spread is

$$c^{T-\text{CDS}} = (1 - R)\lambda.$$

For instance, suppose we consider a CDS traded at 90 bps written on a reference entity with recovery rate $R = 50\%$. We can estimate the probability that the reference entity will default in the next 5 years as follows:

$$\lambda = 0.0090/(1 - 0.5) = 0.018$$

$$P_{\text{Surv}}(t) = \exp(-\lambda t) \approx (1 - \lambda t)$$

$$P_{\text{Def}}(t) = (1 - P_{\text{Surv}}(5y)) \approx \lambda \times 5 = 0.018 \times 5 = 9.0\%.$$

Hence a 90-bp spread corresponds to a 9% (risk-neutral) probability of defaulting within a period of 5 years from time zero.

3.1.2 Calibration Assumptions

Figure 3.4 shows an example of a real market CDS term structure referring to General Motors as of 26 October 2004. The circles in the figure represent the values of the par spread for five CDSs related to General Motors with various times to maturity (1 year, 3 years, 5 years, and 10 years respectively).

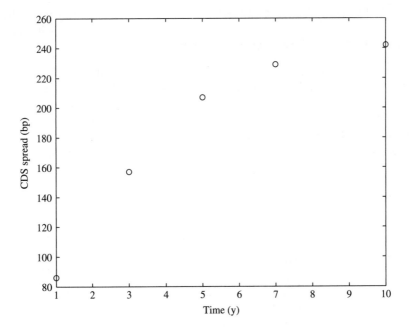

Figure 3.4 CDS term structure for General Motors as of 26 October 2004

This type of data will be used throughout the book in calibration exercises, and models will be calibrated in order to match real market spreads as accurately as possible. Specifically in the calibrations we often minimize the root mean square error (RMSE) given by:

$$\text{RMSE} = \sqrt{\sum_{\text{CDS prices}} \frac{(\text{Market CDS price} - \text{Model CDS price})^2}{\text{Number of CDS prices}}} \qquad (3.7)$$

where the sum over CDS prices refers to the fact that, for the same reference entity, we will consider CDSs with different maturities, as shown in Figure 3.4. Starting from a set of input parameters, a search algorithm looks for the set of parameters minimizing the RMSE. At each step, parameters are changed in a 'clever' way so that the output of the calibration exercise is the set of parameters which best fit market data in RMSE sense.

3.2   CREDIT DEFAULT SWAP FORWARDS

A CDS forward contract is the obligation agreed today to enter a CDS contract on a determined future date t, for a specific spread, called the *forward spread*. We will indicate with $c^{(t,t+T)-\text{Fwd}}$ the forward spread, T being the lifetime of the CDS. In practice, the only difference between a CDS and a CDS forward is that the former starts immediately and covers the protection buyer up to its maturity, while the latter starts on a future date t and protects the owner of the contract over the time period from t to the CDS maturity date $(t + T)$.

3.2.1   Credit Default Swap Forward Pricing

Similar to the CDS, for a CDS forward we look for the forward spread, i.e. the fair spread that makes the forward premium leg equal to the forward loss leg. Consider a discrete time setting $t_i, i = 0, 1, \ldots, n$. The forward is struck at time $t_0 = 0$, and $t_1 = t$ is the date at which the CDS starts. The CDS matures at time $t_n = t + T$ and has a number of payment dates $t_i, i = 2, 3 \ldots, n$, as shown in Figure 3.5.

The forward par spread $c^{(t,t+T)-\text{Fwd}}$ will be such that $\text{PV}_{\text{Fees}}^{(t,t+T)-\text{Fwd}} = \text{PV}_{\text{Loss}}^{(t,t+T)-\text{Fwd}}$, which means that

$$
\begin{aligned}
c^{(t,t+T)-\text{Fwd}} &= \frac{\text{PV}_{\text{Loss}}^{(t,t+T)-\text{Fwd}}}{A(0, t + T) - A(0, t)} \\
&= \frac{\text{PV}_{\text{Loss}}^{(t+T)-\text{CDS}} - \text{PV}_{\text{Loss}}^{t-\text{CDS}}}{A(0, t + T) - A(0, t)} \\
&= \frac{\text{PV}_{\text{Fee}}^{(t+T)-\text{CDS}} - \text{PV}_{\text{Fee}}^{t-\text{CDS}}}{A(0, t + T) - A(0, t)} \\
&= \frac{c^{(t+T)-\text{CDS}} A(0, t + T) - c^{t-\text{CDS}} A(0, t)}{A(0, t + T) - A(0, t)},
\end{aligned}
\qquad (3.8)
$$

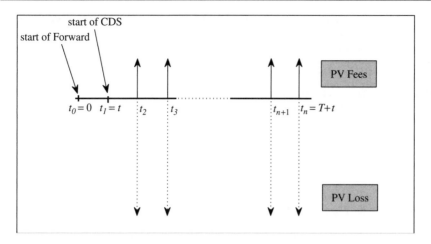

Figure 3.5   CDS forward pricing in discrete times

where $c^{u-\text{CDS}}$ and $A(0, u)$ indicate, respectively, the current spread and the risky annuity of a CDS contract with maturity u. The equalities are based on the fact that over the time interval $(t, t + T)$ the owner of a CDS forward is protected as the owner of a standard CDS, thus the premiums/loss legs of the CDS forward can be seen as the difference between the premium/loss legs of two standard CDSs with maturities t and $(t + T)$, respectively.

3.3   CONSTANT MATURITY CREDIT DEFAULT SWAPS

A single-name Constant Maturity Credit Default Swap (CMCDS) has the same features as a standard single-name CDS. It offers the buyer protection against loss at the event of a default of a reference entity in exchange for a periodically paid spread. The difference is that the spread paid is not fixed but it is floating.

Typically, the spread is reset at prespecified reset dates. At each reset date the CMCDS spread is set to a reference CDS[1] market spread times a multiplier, the so-called *participation rate*. The reference CDS has a maturity which is not necessarily the same as the maturity of the CMCDS.

Example   Consider a 3-year CMCDS with a 5-year single-name CDS as reference. To understand the difference between CDS and CMCDS, we assume that one can now contract a corresponding 3-year CDS for a fixed spread of 84 bps. Assume also that the CMCDS spread is reset quarterly and that the participation rate is $\pi = 80\%$. Table 3.1 shows the CMCDS floating spread (third column) to be paid at each reset date, considering that the par spreads of the 5-year CDS on the same dates are those in column 2.

---

[1] Another option is to choose as reference entity a CDS index.

Table 3.1 Example of computation of a 3-year CMCDS spread (column 3) starting from the par spread of the 5-year CDS (column 2) and comparison with the fixed contracted spread of the corresponding 3-year CDS

Reset dates	5-year CDS par spread (bp)	CMCDS spread, $\pi = 80\%$ (bp)	3-year CDS fixed spread (bp)
3 months	100	80	84
6 months	95	76	84
9 months	120	96	84
12 months	105	84	84
15 months	85	68	84
18 months	115	92	84
21 months	125	100	84
24 months	95	76	84

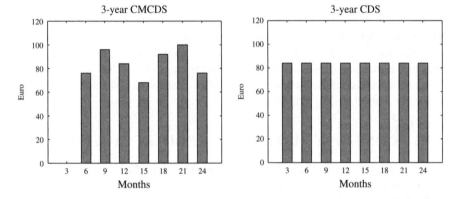

Figure 3.6 Comparison between the protection buyer cash flows of a 3-year CMCDS (left plot) and a 3-year CDS (right plot)

Figure 3.6 plots the cash flows of the protection seller using the spreads in Table 3.1 applied to the case of $N = 10,000$ euros and maturity $T = 3$ years. The left plot refers to the CMCDS, the right one to the case of the standard CDS. In contrast to the fixed premiums of the CDS, the premiums of the CMCDS are fluctuating over time.

3.3.1 Constant Maturity Credit Default Swaps Pricing

Next, we value a CMCDS with maturity $\hat{T}$ and n reset dates $t_i, i = 1, 2, \ldots, n$ (where $t_n = \hat{T}$) with a reference CDS with maturity T. Pricing the CMCDS corresponds to finding the participation rate π which makes the loss leg of the contract equal to the premium leg. However, the loss leg of the CMCDS and the loss leg of a CDS written on the same reference name, and with the same maturity $\hat{T}$, are identical since the two contracts provide for the same protection over the time interval $(0, \hat{T})$. Using Equation (3.1) we get:

$$\text{PV}_{\text{Loss}}^{\hat{T}-\text{CMCDS}} = \text{PV}_{\text{Loss}}^{\hat{T}-\text{CDS}} = (1-R)N \sum_{i=1}^{n} D(0, t_i)(P_{\text{Surv}}(t_{i-1}) - P_{\text{Surv}}(t_i)),$$

$$= N c^{\hat{T}-\text{CDS}} \sum_{i=1}^{n} D(0, t_i) P_{\text{Surv}}(t_i) \Delta t_i,$$

where R denotes the recovery rate, N the notional, $D(0, t_i)$ the discount factor at time t_i and $P_{\text{Surv}}(t_j)$ the survival probability up to the jth reset date. This also implies that the premium legs of the two contracts must be the same ($\text{PV}_{\text{Fees}}^{\hat{T}-\text{CMCDS}} = \text{PV}_{\text{Fees}}^{\hat{T}-\text{CDS}}$).

As detailed in Jönsson and Schoutens (2009), a first approximation to the value of the floating CMCDS premium leg is obtained assuming that the expected reference spread at each reset date equals the forward spread of the same maturity at the time the contract is agreed. The present value of the fees CMCDS leg is thus:

$$\text{PV}_{\text{Fees}}^{\hat{T}-\text{CMCDS}} \simeq \pi N \sum_{i=1}^{n} D(0, t_i) \Delta t_i \, P_{\text{Surv}}(t_i) c^{(t_i, t_i + T) - \text{Fwd}}, \qquad (3.9)$$

where Δt_i is the distance between two consecutive payments, expressed in the appropriate day-count convention, and $c^{(t_i, t_i + T) - \text{Fwd}}$ is the forward CDS spread starting at the reset date t_i with maturity $(t_i + T)$.

By equating the fees leg of the $\hat{T} - \text{CMCDS}$ and the fees leg of the $\hat{T} - \text{CDS}$ we obtain, using Equations (3.1) and (3.9), the participation rate which is given approximately by:

$$\pi \approx \frac{c^{\hat{T}-\text{CDS}} \sum_{i=1}^{n} D(0, t_i) P_{\text{Surv}}(t_i) \Delta t_i}{\sum_{i=1}^{n} D(0, t_i) \Delta t_i \, P_{\text{Surv}}(t_i) c^{(t_i, t_i + T) - \text{Fwd}}}. \qquad (3.10)$$

We need, however, to adjust this approximation since the realized spread at the reset dates are not equal to the forward spreads calculated at the valuation date t_0. The adjustment that has to be added to the premium leg is called the *convexity adjustment* (Nomura 2005). The difficulty in the valuation problem of a CMCDS is exactly this convexity adjustment. This problem is tackled in Jönsson and Schoutens (2009).

3.4   OPTIONS ON CDS

The most common options on CDSs are payer and receiver swaptions. They are the counterparties of the classical European call and put options in other markets. A receiver option holder (i.e. the owner of a CDS call) on a single-name CDS has the right, but not the obligation, to buy risk (i.e. sell the CDS and receive premium) at a predetermined strike spread level at maturity (European option) or prior to maturity (American option). Alternatively, a payer option holder (i.e. the owner of a CDS put) on a single-name CDS has the right, but not the obligation, to sell risk (i.e. buy the CDS and pay premium) at a predetermined strike spread level at maturity (European option) or prior to maturity (American option).

For instance, a European payer option on General Electrics 5 years CDS with maturity $\hat{T} = 1$ year with a spread $c = 25$ bps per year gives the holder the right to buy at maturity protection against the default of General Electrics for 5 years paying a premium of 25 bps. The option will be exercised if the par spread of the 5-year CDS at maturity will be higher than 25 bps (see Figure 3.7).

Special rules apply for the case when default happens before the option's maturity. The most common situation on the single-name payer and receiver structures is a knock-out clause, meaning that, in case of early default, the option is worthless.

Consider a CDS with time to maturity T and a European option on this CDS. Denote the maturity of this option with $\hat{T}$. Denote the fair par spread at time zero of the CDS by $c_0^{T-\text{CDS}}$. This fair spread was calculated by equating premium and

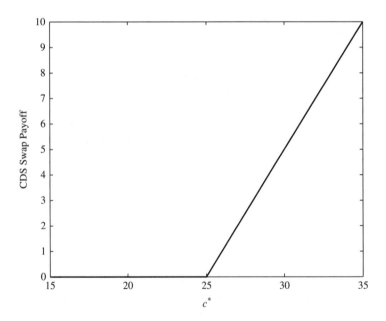

Figure 3.7   Payoff (in bps p.a.) of a CDS swaption with spread $c = 25$ bps as a function of the par spread c^* at maturity

loss legs. For a different spread y, one could also calculate the premium leg. This premium leg equals (assume the notional $N = 1$):

$$y \times A(0, T).$$

Let us write $\mathrm{CDS}_0(y; T)$ for the *price* (to be paid up front to the protection seller when the deal is struck) to enter into a CDS agreement with maturity T and buying protection at time zero for a contract paying y premium. Then

$$\mathrm{CDS}_0(y; T) = \mathrm{PV}_{\mathrm{Loss}}^{T-\mathrm{CDS}} - y \times A(0, T).$$

Note that $\mathrm{CDS}_0(y; T)$ can be positive (in the case $y < c_0^{T-\mathrm{CDS}}$) as well as negative (in the case $y > c_0^{T-\mathrm{CDS}}(T)$). Moreover, we have

$$\mathrm{CDS}_0(c_0^{T-\mathrm{CDS}}; T) = 0.$$

Depending on the evolution of the market, the situation at some time t can be different and hence at that time the price to enter into a similar agreement is stochastic. We denote by $\mathrm{CDS}_t(y; T)$, its time t price and by $c_t^{T-\mathrm{CDS}}$ its time t fair spread. Note that

$$\mathrm{CDS}_t(c_t^{T-\mathrm{CDS}}; T) = 0.$$

For a knock-out receiver (R) and payer (P) with strike spread K and maturity T, the current price of the option is, by risk-neutral valuation theory, given by the discounted expected value of the payoff:

$$\Pi_0^R(\hat{T}, T, K) = \exp(-r\hat{T})\mathbb{E}[(\mathrm{CDS}_{\hat{T}}(c_{\hat{T}}^{T-\mathrm{CDS}}; T) - \mathrm{CDS}_{\hat{T}}(K; T))^+ \mathbf{1}(\tau > \hat{T})]$$

$$= \exp(-r\hat{T})\mathbb{E}[(-\mathrm{CDS}_{\hat{T}}(K; T))^+ \mid \tau > \hat{T}]P_{\mathrm{Surv}}(\hat{T}), \qquad (3.11)$$

$$\Pi_0^P(\hat{T}, T, K) = \exp(-r\hat{T})\mathbb{E}[(\mathrm{CDS}_{\hat{T}}(K; T) - \mathrm{CDS}_{\hat{T}}(c_{\hat{T}}^{T-\mathrm{CDS}}; T))^+ \mathbf{1}(\tau > \hat{T})]$$

$$= \exp(-r\hat{T})\mathbb{E}[(\mathrm{CDS}_{\hat{T}}(K; T))^+ \mid \tau > \hat{T}]P_{\mathrm{Surv}}(\hat{T}) \qquad (3.12)$$

where r is the risk-free rate, $\hat{T}$ is the expiration of the option, τ is the time of default, and $\mathbf{1}(A)$ is the indicator function, which is equal to 1 if the event A is true and 0 otherwise.

Firm-Value Lévy Models

4.1 THE MERTON MODEL

The first firm-value model dates back to Merton (1974) and makes use of a Black–Scholes type model (Black and Scholes 1973) to estimate the survival probability of a reference entity. Starting from the idea that the (financial) assets of a company include equities and liabilities, in this model it is assumed that the asset value of the entity $V = \{V_t, 0 \leq t \leq T\}$ is the sum of the equity value, $E = \{E_t, 0 \leq t \leq T\}$, and the value of a zero-coupon bond $z^T = \{z_t^T, 0 \leq t \leq T\}$ with maturity T and face value L:

$$V_t = E_t + z_t^T.$$

Default occurs if, at maturity, the asset value is not enough to pay back the face value L. In this case the bondholders take control of the firm and the shareholders receive nothing. Conversely, if, at maturity, $V_T \geq L$, default does not occur and the shareholders receive $V_T - L$. These assumptions allow us to treat the firm's equity as a European call option:

$$E_T = \max(V_T - L, 0) = (V_T - L)^+ = \begin{cases} V_T - L & \text{if } V_T \geq L \text{ (no default)} \\ 0 & \text{if } V_T < L \text{ (default).} \end{cases}$$

$$(4.1)$$

Equation (4.1) clearly shows that the shareholders are long a call option on the firm's asset value with strike L and maturity T; on the other hand, debtholders are short a put option on the firm's asset value with strike L and maturity T. This is also schematically presented in Figure 4.1 for a barrier $L = 40$ (we often take $V_0 = 100$).

Following the assumptions of the Black–Scholes model, the dynamics of the asset value $V = \{V_t, 0 \leq t \leq T\}$ is supposed to follow a geometric Brownian motion:

$$V_t = \mu V_t \, dt + \sigma_V V_t \, dW_t \qquad V_0 > 0, \tag{4.2}$$

or equivalently

$$V_t = V_0 \exp \left((\mu - \sigma_V^2) t + \sigma_V W_t \right) \qquad V_0 > 0, \tag{4.3}$$

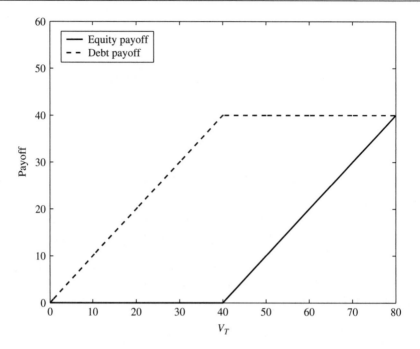

Figure 4.1 Assumption of the Merton model: the asset shareholders are long a call option with strike $L = 40$ and maturity T; the debtholders are short a put option with the same strike and maturity

where μ is the drift parameter, $\sigma_V > 0$ is the asset volatility, and $W = \{W_t, 0 \le t \le T\}$ is a standard Brownian motion. This assumption implies that at any time t the firm asset value is Lognormally distributed: $\log(V_t) - \log(V_0) \sim N(t(\mu - \frac{1}{2}\sigma^2), \sigma^2 t)$.

Figure 4.2 represents two realizations of geometric Brownian motions with drift $\mu = 0.05$, volatility $\sigma_V = 0.4$, and $V_0 = 100$. The paths represent two different behaviours of a reference entity. We will refer to the scenario represented by the dotted line as A; the other realization will be labelled as B. The dashed line is the face value of the zero-coupon bond, L. In the case where the evolution of the reference entity follows the solid path, default occurs at maturity since $V_T^B < L$. On the contrary, if the scenario represented by the dotted path is realized, the reference entity will survive, since $V_T^A > L$. Note that V^A falls below the barrier L before maturity. Nevertheless, default happens only at time T if $V_T^A > L$, no matter if $V_t^A < L$ at any time $t < T$.

Since the equity can be seen as a call option, then, following the Black–Scholes model, the dynamics of the equity under the risk-neutral measure are given by:

$$E_t = V_t \Phi(d_1) - \exp\left(-r(T - t)\right) L \Phi(d_2)$$

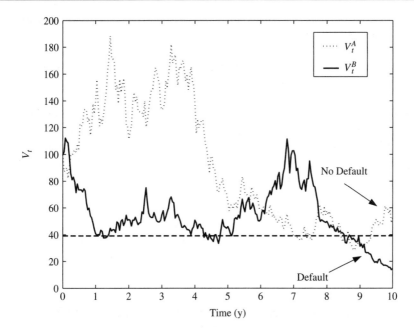

Figure 4.2   Exemplification of the Merton model. The default barrier is set at $L = 40$

where $\Phi(\cdot)$ indicates the distribution function of a Standard Normal random variable and

$$d_1 = \frac{\log(V_t/D) + (r + \sigma_V^2/2)(T - t)}{\sigma_V\sqrt{T - t}}$$

$$d_2 = d_1 - \sigma_V\sqrt{T - t}.$$

At any time $0 \le t \le T$, the (risk-neutral) conditional probability that no default will occur in $(t, T]$ corresponds to the (risk-neutral) probability of finishing in the money for the virtual call option held by the shareholders. Using the results of the Black–Scholes model, this is given by:

$$P_{\text{Surv}}(T|\mathcal{F}_t) = P(V_T > L|\mathcal{F}_t) = \Phi(d_2),$$

where $\mathbb{F} = \{\mathcal{F}_t\}_{t\ge 0}$ is the filtration generated by $V = \{V_t, t \ge 0\}$ and represents the information of the firm's value process up to time t.

It is clear that the main advantage of the Merton model relies in the direct applicability of the Black–Scholes theory. However, the model has many disadvantages:

- First, default can happen only at maturity, no matter the behaviour of the asset value before T. To overcome this weakness, the class of the so-called

first-passage models (e.g. Black and Cox, 1976) have been developed. This class
of model will be treated in Section 4.2.

• Second, the capital structure of a firm is usually much more complicated than
  the one assumed by Merton (a simple zero-coupon bond). Geske (1977, 1979)
  proposed to treat the firm debts as a coupon bond, where default can occur at
  any coupon payment.

• Moreover, the assumption of a constant short rate r has been criticized. Many
  extensions of the Merton model aimed at including a stochastic interest rate have
  been investigated, among which, for instance, Longstaff and Schwartz (1995).
  In our approach we will not consider a stochastic interest rate process.

• Another limitation of the Merton model is the predictability of default. This
  is a consequence of the path continuity of geometric Brownian motion which
  implies that default can be predicted with increasing precision as time passes.
  This weakness is still present in the classic first-passage models based on diffusion processes. A way to introduce a sudden default is the inclusion of jumps in
  the dynamics of the asset value. This issue will be investigated in Section 4.3.

4.2   THE BLACK–COX MODEL WITH CONSTANT BARRIER

As already mentioned in Section 4.1, first-passage models have been introduced in
order to include the possibility of an early default for the reference entity. In fact,
the general hypothesis of first-passage models is that default takes place the first
time the asset value $V = \{V_t, 0 \le t \le T\}$ goes below a default barrier L, which
can be given either exogenously or endogenously with respect to the model.

The pioneer first-passage model, developed by Black and Cox (1976), is a natural extension of the Merton model. The asset value $V = \{V_t, 0 \le t \le T\}$ is still
modelled by a geometric Brownian motion (see Equation (4.2)). However, default
occurs the *first* time $V = \{V_t, 0 \le t \le T\}$ hits the barrier L:

$$\tau = \inf\{t > 0 | V_t \le L\}.$$

Although the Black and Cox (1976) model assumes the barrier to be time dependent,
we will consider a constant barrier L for the sake of the explanation. As in the
Merton model, we can think of L as the face value of the debts of the company.

Figure 4.3 shows two realizations of geometric Brownian motions with drift
$\mu = 0.05$, volatility $\sigma_V = 0.4$ and $V_0 = 100$. The paths represent two possible
behaviours of the reference entity. As in the previous example, we refer to the
scenario represented by the dotted line as A; the other realization is labelled B. In
the case where the evolution follows the solid path, the barrier is hit after around
2 years and a default event occurs. On the contrary, in the case of scenario A, the
reference entity will survive, since $V_t^A > L$ for all $0 \le t \le T$.

Thanks to the properties of Brownian motion, in particular the reflection principle, the distribution of the first hitting time is known (see, for instance, Karatzas

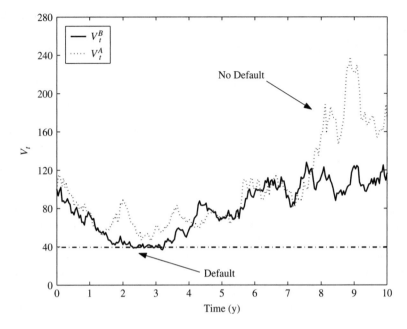

Figure 4.3 Exemplification of a first-passage model

and Shreve 1999). If the underlying asset has survived up to time t, the conditional survival probability up to maturity in the risk-neutral setting is given by:

$$P_{\text{Surv}}(T|\mathcal{F}_t) = P(\tau > T | \tau > t) = \Phi(d_3) - \frac{L}{V_t}^{(2r/\sigma_V^2)-1} \Phi(d_4)$$

where Φ is the distribution function of a Standard Normal random variable and

$$d_3 = \frac{\log(V_t/L) + (r - \sigma_V^2/2)(T - t)}{\sigma_V \sqrt{T - t}}$$
$$d_4 = d_3 - \sigma_V \sqrt{T - t}.$$

This result has been subsequently extended to the situation where the default barrier, say H, is assumed to be lower than the value of the asset's liabilities L. We can think of this hypothesis as if the barrier acts as a protection mechanism for bondholders against an unsatisfactory performance of the company. The asset value can go below L (the company's liabilities) before maturity, but needs to be always higher than this value at maturity. It is said in this situation that the barrier acts as a safety covenant. Default prior to maturity happens when H is hit.

Numerous other extensions and modifications of the Black–Cox model have been developed to include, for instance, stochastic interest rates and a stochastic default barrier (see, e.g., Longstaff and Schwartz 1995, Kim *et al.* 1993). Other generalizations can be found in, for instance, Leland (1994), Leland and Toft (1996) and Anderson and Sundaresan (1996). An extensive review of first-passage models can be found in Bielecki and Rutkowski (2002).

4.3 THE LÉVY FIRST-PASSAGE MODEL

Here we focus on Lévy-based first-passage models under which the asset value process $V = \{V_t, 0 \le t \le T\}$ is described by the exponential of a (non-Brownian) Lévy process. Several models incorporating jumps in the dynamics of the firm value are described in the literature: Zhou (1996, 2001), Hilberink and Rogers (2002), Kou and Wang (2003), Lipton (2002), Cariboni and Schoutens (2007), Kyprianou and Surya (2007), Madan and Schoutens (2008). While Zhou extends the Longstaff and Schwartz (1995) model by considering a Lognormally distributed jump component, Hilberink and Rogers opt for an extension of Leland (1994), using Lévy processes which only allow for downward jumps in the firm's value. It is also important to note the work of Kou and Wang (2003, 2004), in which, as in Lipton (2002), one has shown how to use fluctuation identities from the theory of Lévy processes to price path-dependent options on assets driven by jump diffusions with exponentially distributed Poissonian jumps. The price formulas obtained are also of a relatively simple explicit form when written as functions of the Laplace variable. As in Lipton (2002), Madan and Schoutens (2008) work with downward jumps, and hence allow for situations where the default barrier is not just hit but crossed by a jump. Lipton (2002) considers jump diffusions with finite arrival rates for the jumps. The unit time distribution for such processes is, however, not a limit law allowing for a large number of independent effects on the underlying asset price process. For long-dated contracts Madan and Schoutens (2008) argue that one should use limit laws and set up the theory for laws that are self-decomposable at unit time and are thereby limit laws (Sato 1999). Madan and Schoutens (2008) detail the theory for general spectrally negative Lévy processes and work out in detail some popular examples. In terms of analytics, this will lead us to a contour shift in order get the CDS spreads calculated. Cariboni and Schoutens (2007) detail a general Lévy model and perform the calculations under the VG example. The numerical calculations are based on solving Partial Differential Integral Equations (PDIEs). Zhou (2001) offers a theory that explains observed empirical regularities on default probabilities, recovery rates, and credit spreads by incorporating jump risk into the default process.

Next, we set up the general Lévy default model and in the following sections detail some of the above-mentioned special cases.

We describe the asset value of the firm by a stochastic process $V = \{V_t, 0 \le t \le T\}$ of the form

$$V_t = V_0 \exp(X_t). \tag{4.4}$$

Since, typically, we work in the risk-neutral setting often the drift in the underlying Lévy process is chosen such that $\mathbb{E}[V_t] = V_0 \exp(rt)$.

We define the default event as the first crossing of some predetermined barrier L (which could be given in terms of, for example, debt-per-share, a global recovery on the debt, etc.).

For an initial value of the asset value $V_0 > L$, default is defined to occur when

$$V_t \leq L$$

or, equivalently, if

$$X_t \leq \log(L/V_0). \tag{4.5}$$

The (risk-neutral) survival probability up to time t is given by:

$$
\begin{aligned}
P_{\text{Surv}}(t) &= \mathbb{P}\left(X_s > \log(L/V_0), \text{ for all } 0 \leq s \leq t\right) \\
&= \mathbb{P}\left(\inf_{0 \leq s \leq t} X_s > \log(L/V_0)\right) \\
&= \mathbb{E}\left[\mathbf{1}\left(\inf_{0 \leq s \leq t} X_s > \log(L/V_0)\right)\right] \\
&= \mathbb{E}\left[\mathbf{1}\left(\inf_{0 \leq s \leq t} V_s > L\right)\right]
\end{aligned}
\tag{4.6}
$$

where $\mathbf{1}(A)$ is the indicator function, equal to 1 if the event A is true and 0 otherwise.

Under the above risk-neutral model we would like to price the CDS par spread introduced in Equations (3.4) and (3.5).

The next two sections show how to estimate the par spread, hypothesizing that the underlying Lévy process is either the Variance Gamma process or is based on a single-sided Lévy process such as the Gamma process.

4.4 THE VARIANCE GAMMA MODEL

Let us consider the model introduced in the previous section and hypothesize that the Lévy process $X = \{X_t, t \geq 0\}$ is based on the Variance Gamma (VG) process introduced in Section 2.3.6 of Chapter 2. More precisely, we take

$$X_t = rt + \omega t + Z_t,$$

where $Z = \{Z_t, t \geq 0\}$ is a VG process with parameters σ, ν and θ. Since

$$\mathbb{E}[\exp(Z_t)] = \left(1 - \theta \nu - \frac{1}{2}\sigma^2 \nu\right)^{-t/\nu},$$

in order to have $\mathbb{E}[V_T] = \exp(rT)V_0$, we thus have to set:

$$\omega = v^{-1} \log \left(1 - \theta v - \frac{1}{2}\sigma^2 v \right). \tag{4.7}$$

For the pricing of European equity options under this model, see e.g. Madan *et al.* (1998) or Schoutens (2003). The pricing of American options (using the PDIE approach) for this model is given in Hirsa and Madan (2003).

Following Cariboni and Schoutens (2007), we show how to estimate, under this VG model, the survival probability by relating it to the price of a binary barrier option. The price of this option can be obtained by solving a Partial Differential Integral Equation (PDIE). This technique has been introduced by Hirsa and Madan (2003) to price American options, but can be readily adapted to price various types of barrier options.

Here we will work with *Binary Down-and-Out Barrier* (BDOB) options with maturity T and barrier level L (BDOB(L, T)); this option pays out a unit currency at maturity if the asset value remains above the barrier during the lifetime of the option and zero otherwise:

$$\text{Payoff of BDOB}(L, T) = \begin{cases} 1 & V_t > L, \text{ for all } t, 0 \le t \le T \\ 0 & \text{otherwise}. \end{cases}$$

Under the risk-neutral measure, the price at time $t = 0$ of such an instrument is given by:

$$\text{BDOB}_T = \text{BDOB}(L, T) = \exp(-rT)\mathbb{E}\left[\mathbf{1}\left(\min_{0 \le s \le T} V_s > L \right) \right].$$

Note that, using Equation (4.6), this price becomes:

$$\text{BDOB}_T = \exp(-rT)P_{\text{Surv}}(T) = D(0, T)P_{\text{Surv}}(T),$$

and we can thus rewrite the par spread as, for example, in Equation (3.5) in terms of the binary barrier prices as

$$c^{T-\text{CDS}} = \frac{(1 - R)\left(1 - \text{BDOB}_T - r \int_0^T \text{BDOB}_s \, ds \right)}{\int_0^T \text{BDOB}_s \, ds}, \tag{4.8}$$

where, for simplicity, we have discarded the dependence of the barrier option on (L, T). The problem of calculating the par spread thus reduces to the calculation of the pricing function of a binary *down-and-out barrier* for all maturities up to time T.

The price of the BDOB option with barrier L and time to maturity T is obtained through its link with the price of the corresponding *Binary Down-and-In Barrier* (BDIB) option with equal barrier and maturity. This claim pays out, at maturity, a unit currency if the asset price $V = \{V_t, 0 \le t \le T\}$ goes below the barrier during the lifetime of the option, and zero otherwise:

$$\text{Payoff of BDIB}(L, T) = \begin{cases} 1 & V_t \leq L, 0 \leq t \leq T \\ 0 & \text{otherwise.} \end{cases}$$

Following the same reasoning presented above for the BDIB option, the price at time t of such an instrument is:

$$\text{BDIB}(L, T) = \exp(-rT)\mathbb{E}\left[\mathbf{1}\left(\min_{0 \leq s \leq T} V_s \leq L\right)\right]. \tag{4.9}$$

In the risk-neutral world, the prices of the BDOB and BDIB options with barrier L and time to maturity T are linked by the following relationship:

$$\text{BDIB}(L, T) + \text{BDOB}(L, T) = \exp(-rT).$$

It is thus possible to estimate the price of the BDOB option once the corresponding BDIB option is priced.

To show how to price a BDIB option we first discuss how to price a *European Binary Option* EBO with maturity T. This is a claim with payoff function 1 if the asset value at maturity is below the barrier, and 0 otherwise:

$$\text{Payoff of EBO}(L, T) = \begin{cases} 1 & V_T \leq L \\ 0 & \text{otherwise.} \end{cases}$$

The price of this claim at time $t \leq T$ is given by

$$\text{EBO}_t(L, T) = \exp(-r(T - t))\mathbb{E}\left[\mathbf{1}(V_T \leq L)|\mathcal{F}_t\right],$$

where $\mathbb{F} = \{\mathcal{F}_t\}_{t \geq 0}$ is the filtration generated by the process $V = \{V_t, 0 \leq t \leq T\}$. One can show that the EBO price can be seen as a function of the asset value and the time. For simplicity, we will indicate this function as:

$$\text{EBO}_t(L, T) = F(V_t, t),$$

thus omitting the dependence on (L, T). In the remainder of this section we follow the technique introduced in Hirsa and Madan (2003) to price American options under the VG model. They exploit the fact that the discounted price of an option is a martingale, and hence the infinitesimal generator of the underlying Lévy process (Markov process) applied to this discounted price yields zero. See also Cont and Tankov (2004).

In our case this comes down to:

$$\int_{-\infty}^{+\infty}\left[F(V_{t-}\exp(z), t) - F(V_{t-}, t) - \frac{\partial F}{\partial V}(V_{t-}, t)V_{t-}(\exp(z) - 1)\right]v(dz)$$

$$+ \frac{\partial F}{\partial t}(V_t, t) + rV_t\frac{\partial F}{\partial V}(V_t, t) - rF(V_t, t) = 0,$$

where $v(dz)$ is the Lévy measure of the underlying Lévy process.

By making the change of variables $x = \log(V_t)$ and $\tau = T - t$ and noting

$$w(x, \tau) = F(V_t, t)$$

$$w(x + y, \tau) = F(V_t \exp(y), t)$$

$$\frac{\partial w}{\partial x}(x, \tau) = V_t \frac{\partial F}{\partial V}(V_t, t)$$

$$\frac{\partial w}{\partial \tau}(x, \tau) = -\frac{\partial F}{\partial t}(V_t, t),$$

we obtain the following PDIE, as a function of $w(x, \tau)$,

$$\int_{-\infty}^{+\infty} \left[w(x + y, \tau) - w(x, \tau) - \frac{\partial w}{\partial x}(x, \tau)(\exp(y) - 1) \right] v(dy)$$

$$- \frac{\partial w}{\partial \tau}(x, \tau) + r \frac{\partial w}{\partial x}(x, \tau) - rw(x, \tau) = 0,$$

This PDIE must be solved subject to the initial condition $w(x, 0) = 1$ if $\exp(x) < L$ and zero otherwise.

Noting that $-\omega = \int_{-\infty}^{+\infty} (\exp(y) - 1)v(dy)$, the PDIE can be rewritten as

$$\int_{-\infty}^{+\infty} \left[w(x + y, \tau) - w(x, \tau) \right] v(dy)$$

$$- \frac{\partial w}{\partial \tau}(x, \tau) + (r + \omega) \frac{\partial w}{\partial x}(x, \tau) - rw(x, \tau) = 0. \qquad (4.10)$$

In the appendix of this chapter, we work out a numerical solution for the PDIE, following the scheme presented in Hirsa and Madan (2003) under a VG model. In particular the scheme discretizes the time line and the space of log-asset values via an $N \times M$ grid. To estimate the price of the BDIB option with barrier L and time to maturity T we proceed along the same lines as was done for the European binary option. The only difference is that at each time step, after computing the new values $w_{i,j+1}$ (by solving the above linear system), we impose:

$$w_{i,j+1} = \exp(-(j + 1)r\Delta t) \text{ if } \exp(x_i) < L.$$

By this we ensure that if the barrier L has been crossed, the option will always pay out 1 at maturity.

4.4.1   Sensitivity to the Parameters

This section analyses the sensitivity of the survival probability and the CDS par spread with respect to the parameters describing the VG process. We first vary the kurtosis parameter v keeping all other parameters fixed (see Figure 4.4, top plot). Next, we vary the skewness parameter θ and keep all other parameters fixed (see Figure 4.4, bottom plot). The results are completely in line with our intuitions.

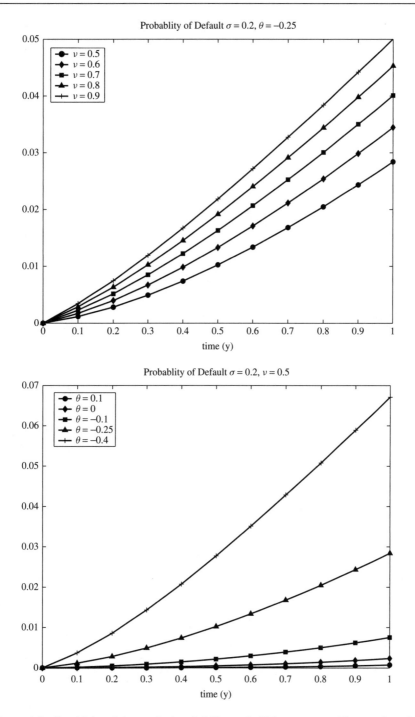

Figure 4.4   Sensitivity of the survival probability to the VG parameters. The top plot refers to the parameter ν, the bottom one to θ

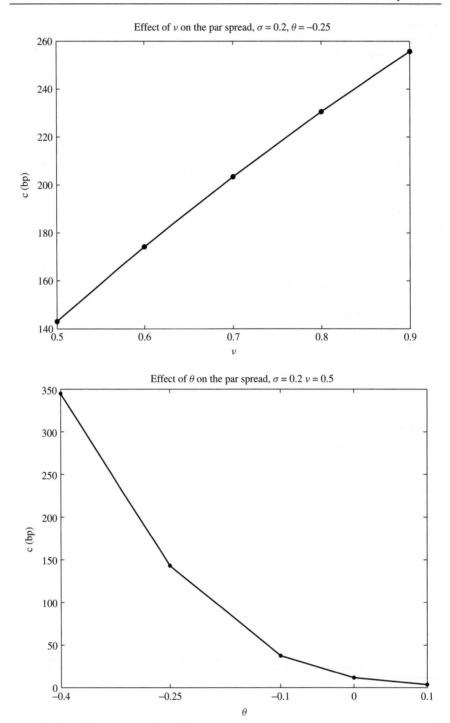

Figure 4.5 Sensitivity of the spread to the VG parameters. The top plot refers to the parameter ν, the bottom one to θ

Higher kurtosis (i.e. higher ν's) give rise to higher default probabilities and higher par spreads (see Figure 4.5, top plot). Also, more negative skewness (i.e. smaller θ's) give the same effect (see Figure 4.5, bottom plot).

4.4.2 Calibration on CDS Term Structure Curve

The performance of the VG Lévy model is tested through a calibration exercise on a series of CDS term structures taken from the market on 26 October 2004. The exercise considers a whole range of differently rated (e.g. the Moody's rating) companies. The short-term rate r is equal to 2.1%, and the recovery rate is fixed to $R = 40\%$ for all the companies.

In Tables 4.1 and 4.2 we report on the results of this calibration exercise. In the former, the optimal VG parameters are given, with the values of the RMSE. In the latter, model estimates are compared with market CDS prices. Figure 4.6 shows an example of calibration for Allstate, where market quotes (circles) are compared with the best fit obtained via the PDIE approach.

Table 4.1 Calibration on CDS (in bps) term structure

Company	σ	ν	θ	RMSE
Mbna Insurance	0.114	2.251	-0.052	2.335
General Elec.	0.011	1.619	-0.084	3.439
Wells Fargo	0.018	2.251	-0.061	3.762
Citigroup	0.032	3.225	-0.048	3.806
Wal-Mart	0.047	0.420	-0.170	2.134
Merrill Lynch	0.145	2.940	-0.001	2.152
Du Pont	0.018	2.868	-0.048	2.069
American Express	0.083	0.564	-0.122	2.621
Allstate	0.065	2.089	-0.067	1.689
Amgen	0.153	3.170	0.002	1.801
McDonald's	0.104	1.291	-0.040	2.329
Ford Credit Co.	0.204	0.964	-0.085	2.674
General Motors	0.083	1.449	-0.150	13.490
Kraft Foods	0.011	1.010	-0.117	2.856
Wyeth	0.011	0.771	-0.172	7.224
Norfolk South.	0.101	0.503	-0.114	3.133
Whirlpool	0.043	1.120	-0.124	8.520
Walt Disney	0.140	0.806	-0.045	1.174
Autozone	0.208	1.011	0.006	3.925
Eastman Kodak	0.212	2.429	-0.007	8.049
Bombardier	0.355	2.813	-0.082	10.621

Table 4.2 Calibration on CDS (in bps) term structure

Company	Moody's		1yr	3yrs	5yrs	7yrs	10yrs
Mbna Insurance	Aaa	Market	21	36	46	51	61
Mbna Insurance	Aaa	Model	21	35	46	53	60
General Elec.	Aaa	Market	5	14	25	29	36
General Elec.	Aaa	Model	7	14	22	29	37
Wells Fargo	Aa1	Market	3	10	20	23	32
Wells Fargo	Aa1	Model	5	10	17	24	33
Citigroup	Aa1	Market	5	12	22	25	34
Citigroup	Aa1	Model	7	12	19	25	35
Wal-Mart	Aa2	Market	1	9	17	22	32
Wal-Mart	Aa2	Model	1	8	17	24	31
Merrill Lynch	Aa3	Market	11	20	31	36	47
Merrill Lynch	Aa3	Model	11	20	30	37	47
Du Pont	Aa3	Market	3	7	13	18	23
Du Pont	Aa3	Model	4	8	12	17	24
American Express	A1	Market	2	12	22	26	36
American Express	A1	Model	3	12	21	28	35
Allstate	A1	Market	12	22	32	37	47
Allstate	A1	Model	12	22	31	38	47
Amgen	A2	Market	14	20	29	34	39
Amgen	A2	Model	13	21	28	34	39
McDonald's	A2	Market	3	10	19	23	34
McDonald's	A2	Model	3	10	18	25	33
Ford Credit Co.	A3	Market	75	154	203	225	238
Ford Credit Co.	A3	Model	75	155	201	225	239
General Motors	A3	Market	86	157	207	229	242
General Motors	A3	Model	90	156	199	227	252
Kraft Foods	A3	Market	4	19	31	40	51
Kraft Foods	A3	Model	6	18	30	40	52
Wyeth	Baa1	Market	15	47	75	85	95
Wyeth	Baa1	Model	18	47	70	85	99
Norfolk South.	Baa1	Market	3	12	28	34	44
Norfolk South.	Baa1	Model	3	14	26	35	44
Whirlpool	Baa1	Market	16	36	66	73	86
Whirlpool	Baa1	Model	17	39	59	74	89
Walt Disney	Baa2	Market	6	21	36	45	56
Walt Disney	Baa2	Model	6	21	35	46	56
Autozone	Baa2	Market	25	65	102	117	127
Autozone	Baa2	Model	24	67	99	117	127
Eastman Kodak	Baa3	Market	54	86	127	143	157
Eastman Kodak	Baa3	Model	51	92	122	142	159
Bombardier	Baa3	Market	320	405	425	425	425
Bombardier	Baa3	Model	322	398	426	432	422

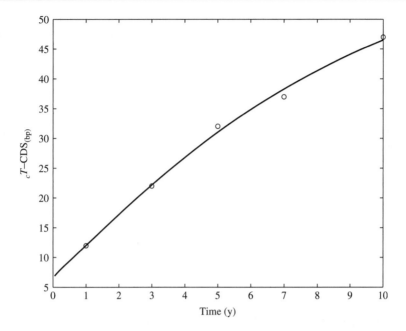

Figure 4.6 Calibrations for Allstate. The circles show the market spreads, the solid bold line is the best fit obtained using the PDIE approach

4.5 ONE-SIDED LÉVY DEFAULT MODEL

4.5.1 Wiener–Hopf Factorization and Default Probabilities

Consider the firm's value in the Lévy model (4.4):

$$V_t = V_0 \exp(X_t), \quad V_0 > 0.$$

where $V = \{V_t, t \geq 0\}$ is the asset value process and hypothesize that the process $X = \{X_t, t \geq 0\}$ is a *spectrally negative* Lévy process (also known as *one-sided negative jump* Lévy processes – i.e. a Lévy process with an upward drift and only negative jumps):

$$X_t = rt + \omega t + Y_t, \tag{4.11}$$

$Y = \{Y_t, t \geq 0\}$ being a pure jump Lévy process with only negative jumps. Examples of spectrally negative Lévy processes are the shifted Gamma process, the shifted CMY process, and the shifted Inverse Gaussian process, introduced respectively in Section 2.3.3, Section 2.3.5, and Section 2.3.4 of Chapter 2.

As detailed in Madan and Schoutens (2008), under this setting it is possible to calculate very efficiently the survival probability $P_{\text{Surv}}(t)$. In order to work in the risk-neutral setting, we have to make the growth rate on the exponential of X equal to the risk-free interest rate, and thus set, in Equation (4.11), $\omega = -\log(\mathbb{E}[\exp(Y_1)])$. Note that $\mu = r + \omega$ is positive and the Lévy measure $\nu(dx)$ in our setting satisfies the integrability condition

$$\int_{-\infty}^{0} \left(|x|^2 \wedge 1\right) \nu(dx) < \infty.$$

In order to apply the methodology described below, which estimates the survival probability via a double inverse Fourier transform, what is needed is that, for large z,

$$\frac{\varphi(z) - \mu z}{z} \to 0. \tag{4.12}$$

Equivalently, by using the Lévy–Khintchine representation, this means that

$$\lim_{z \to \infty} \frac{1}{z} \int_{-\infty}^{0} (\exp(zx) - 1 + z\,(|x| \wedge 1))\, \nu(dx) = 0.$$

This condition is verified for the applications considered in the remainder of this chapter. Since default is triggered by the crossing of a low barrier, or equivalently by the point where the running minimum will cross that level (see also Equation (4.6)), the distribution of the running maximum and minimum of the Lévy process $X = \{X_t, t \geq 0\}$ will be essential in the sequel:

$$\overline{X}_t = \sup_{0 \leq u \leq t} X_u \qquad \text{and} \qquad \underline{X}_t = \inf_{0 \leq u \leq t} X_u.$$

Recall that one can write,

$$\mathbb{E}\left[\exp\left(zX_t\right)\right] = \exp(t\varphi_X(z))$$

where $\varphi_X(z)$ is the so-called *Lévy exponent*.

Let T_λ be an independent exponential random variable with parameter λ. Then the Laplace transform of the process X taken at an exponential time is given by

$$\mathbb{E}\left[\exp\left(zX_{T_\lambda}\right)\right] = \frac{\lambda}{\lambda - \varphi_X(z)}.$$

For this expression we have the remarkable Wiener–Hopf factorization (Rogozin 1996), which is valid for general Lévy processes:

$$\frac{\lambda}{\lambda - \varphi_X(z)} = \varphi_\lambda^+(z)\varphi_\lambda^-(z)$$

$$= \mathbb{E}\left[\exp\left(z\overline{X}_{T_\lambda}\right)\right]\mathbb{E}\left[\exp\left(z\underline{X}_{T_\lambda}\right)\right].$$

In other words, the Laplace transform of the process X at an independent exponential time factorizes into the Laplace transforms of the running minimum and the running maximum taken at an exponential time. The factors $\varphi_\lambda^-(z)$ and $\varphi_\lambda^+(z)$, which are unique, are called the (left and right) Wiener–Hopf factors.

Moreover, classical Lévy process theory (see, for example, Bertoin 1996, Sato 1999, or Kyprianou 2006) shows that for a spectrally negative process the right Wiener–Hopf factor equals

$$\varphi_\lambda^+(z) = \frac{\beta^*}{\beta^* - z},$$

where β^* is a constant depending on $\lambda : \beta^* = \beta^*(\lambda)$, and that β^* is a solution to

$$\varphi_X(\beta) = \lambda.$$

In other words, the running maximum at an exponential time (with parameter λ) is exponentially distributed with parameter $\beta^* = \varphi_X^{[-1]}(\lambda)$.

It follows that

$$\varphi_\lambda^-(z) = \frac{\lambda}{\lambda - \varphi_X(z)} \frac{\beta^* - z}{\beta^*}.$$

Now note that by partial integration

$$\varphi_\lambda^-(z) = \int_{t=0}^{t=\infty} \int_{x=-\infty}^{x=0} \lambda \exp(-\lambda t) \exp(zx) f_{\underline{X}_t}(x)\, dx\, dt$$

$$= \int_{t=0}^{t=\infty} \int_{x=-\infty}^{x=0} \lambda \exp(-\lambda t) \exp(zx) z P(\underline{X}_t > x)\, dx\, dt$$

$$= \lambda z \int_{t=0}^{t=\infty} \int_{x=-\infty}^{x=0} \exp(-\lambda t) \exp(zx) P(\underline{X}_t > x)\, dx\, dt$$

$$= \frac{\lambda}{\lambda - \varphi_X(z)} \frac{\beta^* - z}{\beta^*}$$

Let us now focus on the time at which the running minimum crosses a barrier x for the first time, that is,

$$\tau_x = \inf\{t : X_t < x\}$$

then we have that $f(t, x)$ – by which we denote the probability that the minimum stays above negative x in t units of time – is:

$$f(t, x) = \mathbb{P}(\tau_{-x} > t) = \mathbb{P}(\underline{X}_t > -x).$$

Hence, we observe the double Laplace transform of f:

$$
\begin{aligned}
g(\lambda, z) &= \int_{t=0}^{t=\infty} \int_{x=0}^{x=\infty} \exp(-\lambda t - zx) f(t, x) \, dx \, dt \\
&= \int_{t=0}^{t=\infty} \int_{x=-\infty}^{x=0} \exp(-\lambda t + zx) \mathbb{P}\left(\underline{X}_t > x\right) \, dx \, dt \\
&= \frac{\beta^*(\lambda) - z}{(\lambda - \varphi_X(z)) \, \beta^*(\lambda) z}.
\end{aligned}
$$

As shown in Madan and Schoutens (2008) it is possible, starting from this equation, to show that $f(t, x)$, the probability that the minimum stays above negative x in t units of time, can be obtained by the following double inverse Fourier transform:

$$
f(t, x) = -\frac{1}{(2\pi)^2} \int_{\Gamma_1} \int_{\Gamma_2} \exp(\lambda t + zx) \frac{\beta^*(\lambda) - z}{(\lambda - \varphi_X(z)) \, \beta^*(\lambda) z} \, d\lambda \, dz,
$$

where the contour $\Gamma_1 = \{\lambda_1 + i\lambda_2 | \lambda_2 = -\infty \cdots + \infty)\}$ and the contour $\Gamma_2 = \{z_1 + iz_2 | z_2 = -\infty \cdots + \infty)\}$.

This can be solved by making a contour change following Rogers (2000) and using the so-called Abate and Whitt approximation for fixed t and x:

$$
\begin{aligned}
S_N = \frac{h_1 h_2}{4\pi^2} \sum_{n=-N}^{N} \sum_{m=-N}^{N} & h'(a_1 + inh_1) \, g(h(a_1 + inh_1), a_2 + imh_2) \\
& \times \exp\{h(a_1 t + inh_1) + x(a_2 + imh_2)\},
\end{aligned}
$$

where i is the imaginary unit, $h(\lambda) = \varphi(\lambda/\mu)$ and $h'(\lambda)$ its derivative.

In Madan and Schoutens (2008), it is suggested to take

$$
\begin{aligned}
a_1 &= \frac{A_1}{2tl_1} \quad \text{and} \quad a_2 = \frac{A_2}{2xl_2} \\
h_1 &= \frac{\pi}{tl_1} \quad \text{and} \quad h_2 = \frac{\pi}{xl_2} \\
A_1 &= A_2 = 22 \\
l_1 &= l_2 = 1 \\
N &= 12
\end{aligned}
$$

Finally, it is recommended to take an Euler summation

$$
f(t, x) \stackrel{\circ}{=} \sum_{k=0}^{M} 2^{-M} \binom{M}{k} S_{N+k} \tag{4.13}
$$

with, for example, $M = 15$.

4.5.2 Illustration of the Pricing of Credit Default Swaps

The approach described in the previous section can be used to price CDSs. We focus on three special cases of spectrally negative Lévy processes given by the shifted Gamma (SG) process, the shifted CMY (SCMY) process, and the shifted inverse Gaussian (SIG) process. For these processes the Lévy exponent and the function $h(\lambda)$ are reported in Table 4.3. Survival probabilities are obtained by using Equation (4.13) and corresponding spreads are computed using Equation (4.3).

The models are calibrated on CDS market spreads, minimizing the absolute error between model CDS quotes and market CDS quotes. As a data set, we use the weekly data from all the 125 companies on the iTraxx over the year 2005. So, we have 125 CDS curves for 52 weeks, making in total 6,500 CDS curves with spread rates of 1, 3, 5, 7 and 10-year maturities. In Table 4.4, one finds a comparison of the mean error over the 125 components for the different maturities together with the total error and the average error per quote for the calibration on the data set of 5 January 2005.

In Figure 4.7, the fit obtained under the different models for Electrolux AB on that day is presented (○ signs are market prices and + signs are calibrated model prices). The SCMY model outperforms the SG and SIG, but also for the two latter models the fit is very acceptable.

Figure 4.8 focuses on the time-evolution of the fits by showing (see keys to figures) the average errors per quote over the 52 weeks for the SIG, SCMY model, and the SG model. As expected, SCMY outperforms SG and SIG. Note that the peak around week 20 corresponds to the autocorrelation crisis of May 2005. Since

Table 4.3 Lévy exponent and $h(\lambda)$ for the the shifted gamma, shifted inverse Gaussian, and shifted CMY processes

Model	$\varphi(z)$	$h(\lambda)$
SG	$\mu z - a \log\left(1 + \frac{z}{b}\right)$	$\lambda - a \log\left(1 + \frac{\lambda}{\mu b}\right)$
SIG	$\mu z - a(\sqrt{2z + b^2} - b)$	$\lambda - a(\sqrt{2\lambda\mu^{-1} + b^2} - b)$
SCMY	$\mu z + C\Gamma(-Y)((M + z)^Y - M^Y)$	$\lambda + C\Gamma(-Y)((M + \lambda\mu^{-1})^Y - M^Y)$

Table 4.4 Mean absolute error (in bps) for calibrations of different models on the 125 CDS in iTraxx on 5 January 2005

Model	1 y	3 y	5 y	7 y	10 y	Total	Average per quote
SG	3.2088	0.6302	1.4056	0.0274	2.9150	8.1870	1.6374
SIG	2.8384	0.5689	1.3062	0.0280	2.7926	7.5342	1.5068
SCMY	1.4187	0.2203	0.6710	0.2262	1.4836	4.0199	0.8040

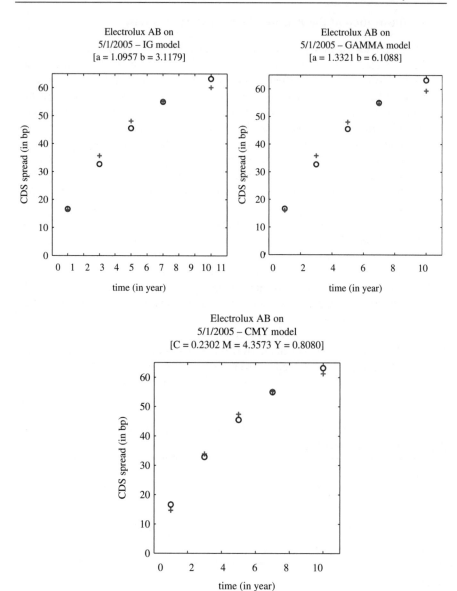

Figure 4.7 Fit for Electrolux on 5 January 2005 under the SIG (top left plot), SG (top right plot) and SCMY (bottom plot) models

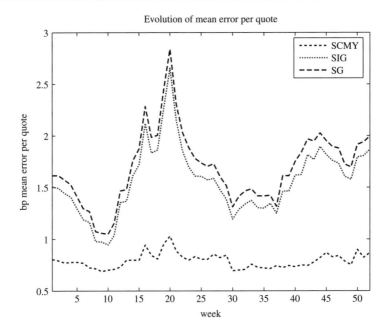

Figure 4.8   Evolution over time of the average calibration error per quote of SG, SIG and SCMY on iTraxx in 2005

we are working with absolute errors, the peak does not necessarily correspond to a worsening fit since, during that period, the average spread went up dramatically. For the SCMY model, the evolution of the mean absolute error over time for each maturity is shown in Figure 4.9.

4.6   DYNAMIC SPREAD GENERATOR

4.6.1   Generating Spread Paths

Having fast CDS pricers based on firm-value models, one can set up a dynamic credit spread generator. Such a dynamic spread generator can be used to price other types of credit derivatives like CMSs or options on CDSs.

We illustrate this procedure here for the single-sided models presented in the previous section, but the procedures can be readily adapted to, for example, the VG model or other double-sided models. Details of the procedure can be found in Jönsson and Schoutens (2008 and 2009). In Jönsson and Schoutens (2009), the dynamic spread generator is used to price Constant Maturity Credit Default Swaps (CMCDSs).

For example, to generate spreads, we introduce stochasticity in the firm-value process. Keeping the default barrier fixed, if the firm-value process is increasing, the distance to the default barrier is bigger and hence the probability of hitting

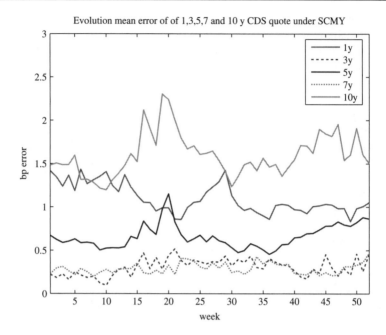

Figure 4.9 Evolution over time of the average calibration error per maturity of SCMY on iTraxx in 2005

it decreases. Recalculating spreads with these lower default probabilities gives a lower spread. If the firm value decreases, one gets closer to the default barrier. The default probability hence increases which translates in higher spreads. Fluctuations in the firm's value hence translates in fluctuations in the default probabilities, which in their turn translates in fluctuations in the fair spreads.

To be more precise, the following steps need to be taken:

1. Calibrate the model on a given term structure of market spreads. In this way the optimal parameters which best fit the market spreads are obtained.
2. Using the default barrier assumed in the calibration, recalculate CDS spread for different initial firm-values V_0. More precisely, take a fine grid of initial firm asset values $\{v_1, v_2, \ldots, v_k\}$, precalculate using the optimal parameters and via Equation (4.13) the corresponding survival probabilities and spreads $\{c_1^{T-\text{CDS}}, c_2^{T-\text{CDS}}, \ldots, c_k^{T-\text{CDS}}\}$. Note that if the new start value $v_i < V_0$, this will lead to a typically higher spread and default probabilities because, from the start, one is already closer by the default barrier. When, $v_i > V_0$ one has the opposite situation.
3. Generate a firm's asset value path on a time grid $\{t_1, t_2, \ldots, t_n\}$, $\widetilde{V} = \{\widetilde{V}_t, t = t_1, \ldots, t_n\}$. For each point in the time grid the corresponding spread is obtained by interpolating $\widetilde{V}_{t_j}$ on $\{v_1, v_2, \ldots, v_k\}$ and in its corresponding $\{c_1^{T-\text{CDS}}, c_2^{T-\text{CDS}}, \ldots, c_k^{T-\text{CDS}}\}$ values.

Note that, going into the implementation details, it turns out that it is often computationally more efficient to set up a grid for the barriers and think in terms of percentage distance to default. For example, a situation $V_0 = 100$ and $L = 50$ has a percentage distance to default of $(100 - 50)/100 = 50\%$. A situation $V_0 = 150, L = 50$ has a percentage distances to default of $(150 - 50)/150 = 66.67\%$. Increasing the firm's value hence increase the percentage distance to default. However the situation $V_0 = 100$ and $L = 33.33$ has also the same percentage distance to default of $(100 - 33.33)/100 = 66.67\%$; lowering the barrier increases the distance. Because actually only this percentage distance to default is determining the default probabilities (default probabilities only depend on the ratio of V_0 and L as can be seen from Equation (4.5)), one can also just set up a grid of different barrier values and calculate for these default probabilities and spreads. Then, for the different barrier values in the grid, one can calculate percentage distances to default and translate these into a grid of initial values for the firm.

In Figure 4.10, we see a path of a firm's value process under the Shifted Gamma model and its corresponding spread evolution. The parameters of the Gamma model are obtained by a calibration of the spread structure of BAE Systems on 5 January 2005 ($a = 1.2028$ and $b = 5.9720$).

Once a fast spread generator is implemented, we are set to price by Monte Carlo methods all kinds of (exotic) European structures on the evolution of the spread of a single-name CDS. In the next section we will illustrate this by pricing options on CDSs.

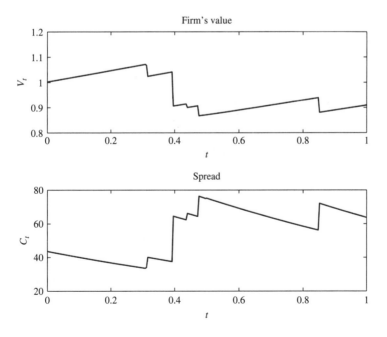

Figure 4.10 Spread path – BAE Systems. Underlying model is the Shifted Gamma with $a = 1.2028$ and $b = 5.9720$. Spot par spread $C_0 = 43$

4.6.2 Pricing of Options on CDSs

Using the dynamic spread generator just introduced, it is possible to price receiver and payer options on a CDS, using Equations (3.11) and (3.12) in Chapter 3. Let us rewrite these equations using a notation which makes reference to the fact that we are working under a firm-value model. Let us denote with

$$c_0^{T-\text{CDS}} = c_0^{T-\text{CDS}}(V_0, R, r, T, \theta)$$

the par spread of a CDS with maturity T at time $t = 0$. The notation stresses that the value of the spreads depends upon the firm's initial value V_0, the recovery rate R, the risk-free rate r, and the vector of parameters θ describing the underlying Lévy process. Similarly, the price to enter into a CDS agreement at time zero for a contract paying c premium can be denoted by:

$$\text{CDS}_0^{T-\text{CDS}}(c) = \text{CDS}_0^{T-\text{CDS}}(V_0, R, r, T, \theta, c).$$

Note that $\text{CDS}_0^{T-\text{CDS}}(V_0, R, r, T, \theta, c_0^{T-\text{CDS}}) = 0$.

Consider a European option on a CDS with maturity T^*. Its payoff depends on the spread value at T^* and, in general, the payoff can depend on the full evolution of the spread until the option's maturity. For this reason let us denote the spread price and the so-called upfront price for a spread c at time t by:

$$c_t^{T-\text{CDS}} = c_t^{T-\text{CDS}}(V_t, R, r, T, \theta), t \geq 0$$

$$\text{CDS}_t^{T-\text{CDS}}(c) = \text{CDS}_t^{T-\text{CDS}}(V_t, R, r, T, \theta, c).$$

Again, we have $\text{CDS}_t^{T-\text{CDS}}(V_t, R, r, T, \theta, c_t^{T-\text{CDS}}) = 0$. For simplicity of notation, let us drop the superscript $T-\text{CDS}$ for the remainder of this section.

Let us write $F(\{\text{CDS}_t, 0 \leq t \leq T^*\}, 1(\tau < T^*))$ for the payoff function to indicate that it depends on the full path of the upfront (or equivalently the spread) and on whether default occurred before maturity or not. Following this notation, the prices of the receiver and payer options with maturity T^* and spread K given by Equations (3.11) and (3.12) become:

$$\Pi_0^R(T^*, K) = \exp(-rT^*)\mathbb{E}[(\text{CDS}_{T^*}(V_{T^*}, R, r, T, \theta, c_{T^*})$$
$$- \text{CDS}_{T^*}(V_{T^*}, R, r, T, \theta, K))^+ 1(\tau > T^*)]$$
$$= \exp(-rT^*)\mathbb{E}[(-\text{CDS}_{T^*}(V_{T^*}, R, r, T, \theta, K))^+ | \tau > T^*] P_{\text{Surv}}(T^*)$$

$$\Pi_0^P(T^*, K) = \exp(-rT^*)\mathbb{E}[(\text{CDS}_{T^*}(V_{T^*}, R, r, T, \theta, K)$$
$$- \text{CDS}_{T^*}(V_{T^*}, R, r, T, \theta, c_{T^*}))^+ 1(\tau > T^*)]$$
$$= \exp(-rT^*)\mathbb{E}[(\text{CDS}_{T^*}(V_{T^*}, R, r, T, \theta, K))^+ | \tau > T^*] P_{\text{Surv}}(T^*).$$

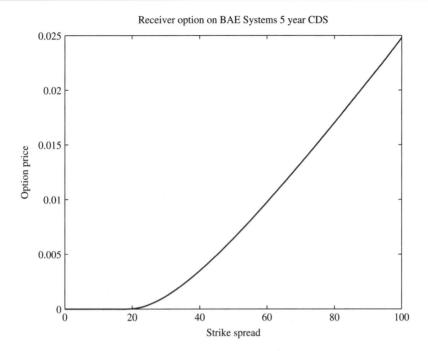

Figure 4.11 One-year receiver option prices – Shifted Gamma model – BAE Systems CDS with 5-year maturity. Underlying model is the Shifted Gamma with $a = 1.2028$ and $b = 5.9720$

The expected values in the above equations can be easily estimated via Monte Carlo simulation using the dynamic spread generator: the evolution of the asset value is mapped back into the evolution of the spread.

In Figure 4.11 one finds the prices for 1-year receiver options on the BAE Systems CDS with 5-year maturity for a whole range of strike spreads calculated using the Shifted Gamma model with optimal parameters $a = 1.2028$ and $b = 5.9720$ given by calibrating the model to the BAE Systems spread term structure on 5 January 2005. The spot (par) spread and the forward spread was $c_0 = 43$ and 47 basis points, respectively.

4.6.3 Black's Formulas and Implied Volatility

The market standard for pricing options on CDSs is Black's model, which is based on the assumption that the credit spread follows a geometric Brownian motion. The Black formulas for payer and receiver swaptions with maturity T^* (see Hull and White 2003) are, respectively:

$$\Pi_0^P(T^*, K)_{BS} = A_0(T^*, T)(c^{(T^*, T^*+T)-Fwd}\Phi(d_1) - K\Phi(d_2))$$
$$\Pi_0^R(T^*, K)_{BS} = A_0(T^*, T)(K\Phi(-d_2) - c^{(T^*, T^*+T)-Fwd}\Phi(-d_1)),$$

where T is the CDS maturity, Φ is the distribution function for a random variable X that is Standard Normally distributed, $c^{(t,t+T)-\text{Fwd}}$ is the present value of a forward spread given by Equation (3.8), $A_0(T^*, T)$ is the so-called *forward risky annuity* given by $A_0(T^*, T) = (A(0, T) - A(0, T^*))$ (see Equation (3.2)), and finally

$$d_1 = \frac{\log(c^{(T^*,T^*+T)-\text{Fwd}}/K) + \sigma^2 T^*/2}{\sigma\sqrt{T^*}}$$

$$d_2 = d_1 - \sigma\sqrt{T^*}.$$

Given the forward spread and risky annuities we can calculate the implied volatilities for payers and receivers written on the same underlying CDS with different strikes, which are reported in Table 4.5 and Table 4.6, respectively. We have assumed a flat term structure of interest rates of 3%. The values of the options are generated using a Shifted Gamma model.

Table 4.5 The estimated values of a European payer with maturity 0.25 year to enter into a single-name CDS (BAE Systems) with a 5-year maturity and the corresponding Black's implied volatilities. The forward spread is 47 bps. The parameters of the underlying Shifted Gamma model are $a = 1.2028$ and $b = 5.9720$

Strike (bp)	Payer	Implied vol (%)
40.0	0.003710	42.4
42.0	0.003414	52.0
44.0	0.003164	59.1
46.0	0.002948	64.8
48.0	0.002758	69.7
50.0	0.002589	73.9

Table 4.6 The estimated values of a European receiver with maturity 0.25 year to enter into a single-name CDS (BAE Systems) with a 5-year maturity and the corresponding Black's implied volatilities. The forward spread is 47 bps. The parameters of the underlying Shifted Gamma model are $a = 1.2028$ and $b = 5.9720$

Strike (bp)	Receiver	Implied vol (%)
40.0	0.001025	57.9
42.0	0.001636	65.3
44.0	0.002293	71.4
46.0	0.002984	76.6
48.0	0.003702	81.3
50.0	0.004440	85.4

APPENDIX: SOLUTION OF THE PDIE

This appendix solves the partial integral differential Equation (4.10). In the finite difference discretization of Equation (4.10), a mixed approach is used. For the evaluation of the jumps term, the integrand is expanded near its singularity at zero and this part is treated implicitly. The rest of the integral is instead treated explicitly, in order for the scheme to be computationally affordable. On the rest of the PDIE, a fully implicit approach is used.

We consider M equally spaced subintervals in the τ direction. For the x direction we assume N equally spaced sub intervals on $[x_{\min}, x_{\max}]$. Denoting by

$$\Delta x = (x_{\max} - x_{\min})/N \quad \text{and} \quad \Delta \tau = T/M,$$

this leads to the following mesh on $[x_{\min}, x_{\max}] \times [0, T]$:

$$D = \{(x_i, \tau_j) \in \mathbb{R}^+ \times \mathbb{R}^+ | x_i = x_{\min} + i \Delta x,$$
$$i = 0, 1, \dots, N; \tau_j = j \Delta \tau, j = 0, 1, \dots, M\}.$$

Let $w_{i,j}$ be the discrete value of $w(x_i, \tau_j)$ on D. Using the first-order finite difference approximation for $\partial w/\partial \tau$ and central difference for $\partial w/\partial x$, we obtain the following discrete equation at point (x_i, τ_{j+1}):

$$\int_{-\infty}^{+\infty} \left[w(x_i + y, \tau_j) - w(x_i, \tau_j) \right] \nu(dy) - \frac{1}{\Delta \tau} (w_{i,j+1} - w_{i,j})$$

$$+ (r + \omega) \frac{1}{2\Delta x} (w_{i+1,j+1} - w_{i-1,j+1}) - r w_{i,j+1} = 0. \tag{4.14}$$

Equivalently,

$$(r + \omega) \frac{\Delta \tau}{2\Delta x} w_{i-1,j+1} - (r + \omega) \frac{\Delta \tau}{2\Delta x} w_{i+1,j+1} + (1 + r\Delta \tau) w_{i,j+1}$$

$$= w_{i,j} + \Delta \tau \int_{-\infty}^{+\infty} \left[w(x_i + y, \tau_j) - w(x_i, \tau_j) \right] \nu(dy) \tag{4.15}$$

where $w_{i,0} = 1$ if $\exp(x_i) < K$, and zero otherwise.

For the evaluation of the jump integral we use an analytical approach to the singularity at zero combined with an explicit approach. We divide it into six integrals, respectively, given by A_1, A_2, A_3, A_4, A_5 and A_6:

$$\int_{-\infty}^{+\infty} \left[w(x_i + y, \tau_j) - w(x_i, \tau_j) \right] k(dy) = \int_{-\infty}^{x_{\min} - x_i} \left[w(x_i + y, \tau_j) - w(x_i, \tau_j) \right] \nu(dy)$$

$$+ \int_{x_{\min} - x_i}^{-\Delta x} \left[w(x_i + y, \tau_j) - w(x_i, \tau_j) \right] \nu(dy)$$

$$+ \int_{-\Delta x}^{0} \left[w(x_i + y, \tau_j) - w(x_i, \tau_j) \right] \nu(dy)$$

$$+ \int_0^{\Delta x} \left[w(x_i + y, \tau_j) - w(x_i, \tau_j) \right] v(dy)$$

$$+ \int_{\Delta x}^{x_{\max} - x_i} \left[w(x_i + y, \tau_j) - w(x_i, \tau_j) \right] v(dy)$$

$$+ \int_{x_{\max} - x_i}^{\infty} \left[w(x_i + y, \tau_j) - w(x_i, \tau_j) \right] v(dy)$$

$$= A_1 + A_2 + A_3 + A_4 + A_5 + A_6 \qquad (4.16)$$

Denoting with

$$\exp \mathrm{int}(x) = \int_x^{\infty} \frac{\exp(-y)}{y} \, dy,$$

the exponential integral function, we have, by following Hirsa and Madan (2003):

$$A_1 \cong v^{-1}(\exp(-r\tau_j) - w_{i,j})\exp \mathrm{int}(i \Delta x \lambda_n)$$

$$A_2 \cong \sum_{k=1}^{i-1} v^{-1}[w_{i-k,j} - w_{i,j} - k(w_{i-k-1,j} - w_{i-k,j})][\exp \mathrm{int}(k \Delta x \lambda_n)$$

$$- \exp \mathrm{int}((k + 1)\Delta x \lambda_n)] + \sum_{k=1}^{i-1} (\lambda_n v \Delta x)^{-1} (w_{i-k-1,j} - w_{i-k,j})$$

$$\times (\exp(-\lambda_n k \Delta x) - \exp(-\lambda_n (k + 1)\Delta x))$$

$$A_3 \cong (v \Delta x \lambda_n)^{-1}(1 - \exp(-\lambda_n \Delta x))(w_{i-1,j} - w_{i,j})$$

$$A_4 \cong (v \Delta x \lambda_p)^{-1}(1 - \exp(-\lambda_p \Delta x))(w_{i+1,j} - w_{i,j})$$

$$A_5 \cong \sum_{k=1}^{N-i-1} v^{-1}[w_{i+k,j} - w_{i,j} - k(w_{i+k+1,j} - w_{i+k,j})][\exp \mathrm{int}(k \Delta x \lambda_p)$$

$$- \exp \mathrm{int}((k + 1)\Delta x \lambda_p)] + \sum_{k=1}^{N-i-1} (\lambda_p v \Delta x)^{-1} (w_{i+k+1,j} - w_{i+k,j})$$

$$\times (\exp(-\lambda_p k \Delta x) - \exp(-\lambda_p (k + 1)\Delta x))$$

$$A_6 \cong v^{-1} w_{i,j} \exp \mathrm{int}((N - i)\Delta x \lambda_p),$$

since, for $y \in (-\infty, x_{\min} - x_i)$, we have $w(x_i + y, t_j) \cong \exp(-rt)$ and for $y \in (x_{\max} - x_i, \infty)$, we have $w(x_i + y, t_j) \cong 0$.

Putting all the pieces together, we obtain the following difference equation at the points (x_i, τ_{j+1}):

$$A w_{i-1,j+1} + B_i w_{i,j+1} - C w_{i+1,j+1} = w_{i,j} + v^{-1} \Delta \tau R_{i,j}, \qquad (4.17)$$

where

$$A = (r + \omega)\frac{\Delta\tau}{2\Delta x} - (1 - \exp(-\lambda_n \Delta x))\frac{\Delta\tau}{\nu \Delta x \lambda_n}$$

$$B_i = 1 + r\Delta\tau + (1 - \exp(-\lambda_n \Delta x))\frac{\Delta\tau}{\nu \Delta x \lambda_n} + (1 - \exp(-\lambda_p \Delta x))\frac{\Delta\tau}{\nu \Delta x \lambda_p}$$

$$+ \frac{\Delta\tau}{\nu}\left(\exp\mathrm{int}(i\Delta x\lambda_n) + \exp\mathrm{int}((N - i)\Delta x\lambda_p)\right)$$

$$C = (r + \omega)\frac{\Delta\tau}{2\Delta x} + (1 - \exp(-\lambda_p \Delta x))\frac{\Delta\tau}{\nu \Delta x \lambda_p}$$

$$R_{i,j} = \sum_{k=1}^{i-1}(w_{i-k,j} - w_{i,j} - k(w_{i-k-1,j} - w_{i-k,j}))(\exp\mathrm{int}(k\Delta x\lambda_n)$$

$$- \exp\mathrm{int}((k+1)\Delta x\lambda_n)) + \sum_{k=1}^{i-1}(\lambda_n \Delta x)^{-1}(w_{i-k-1,j} - w_{i-k,j})$$

$$\times (\exp(-\lambda_n k\Delta x) - \exp(-\lambda_n(k+1)\Delta x))$$

$$+ \sum_{k=1}^{N-i-1}(w_{i+k,j} - w_{i,j} - k(w_{i+k+1,j} - w_{i+k,j}))(\exp\mathrm{int}(k\Delta x\lambda_p)$$

$$- \exp\mathrm{int}((k+1)\Delta x\lambda_p)) + \sum_{k=1}^{N-i-1}(\lambda_p \Delta x)^{-1}(w_{i+k+1,j} - w_{i+k,j})$$

$$\times (\exp(-\lambda_p k\Delta x) - \exp(-\lambda_p(k+1)\Delta x)) + \exp(-r\tau_j)\exp\mathrm{int}(i\Delta x\lambda_n)$$

Assuming that at time τ_j we know the values $w_{i,j}$, we compute for time τ_{j+1} the values $w_{i,j+1}$ by solving the above (tridiagonal) linear system. We always impose the boundary conditions when $i = 1$ or $i = N$.

5

Intensity Lévy Models

5.1 INTENSITY MODELS FOR CREDIT RISK

Intensity-based models, known also as *hazard rate* or *reduced-form* models, focus directly on modelling the default probability. The basic idea lies in the fact that at any instant there is a probability that an obligor will default, which depends on its overall *health*. This probability is assumed to be modelled via a counting process $N = \{N_t, 0 \leq t \leq T\}$ with intensity $\lambda = \{\lambda_t, 0 \leq t \leq T\}$, which thus determines the price of credit risk. In fact, default is assumed to occur at the first jump time of the counting process $N = \{N_t, 0 \leq t \leq T\}$.

The intensity can be deterministic or stochastic and models the default rate for the reference entity. Under this setting the time of default τ can be thought of as a stopping time, i.e. a random variable whose occurrence can be observed at each point in time. To understand the meaning of the default intensity, assume that the reference entity has survived up to time t and let us indicate with τ the default time. The intensity of default is defined as:

$$\lambda_t = \lim_{h \to 0} \frac{\mathbb{P}(t < \tau \leq t + h | \tau > t)}{h}. \tag{5.1}$$

This equation tells us that, roughly speaking, for a small time interval $\Delta t > 0$:

$$\mathbb{P}(\tau \leq t + \Delta t | \tau > t) \approx \lambda_t \Delta t.$$

In the remainder of this section we will present some intensity-based models, starting with a deterministic default intensity and moving subsequently to stochastic diffusion models for $\lambda = \{\lambda_t, 0 \leq t \leq T\}$.

5.1.1 Jarrow–Turnbull Model

Homogeneous Case. A standard example of counting process is the homogeneous Poisson (HP) process with constant default intensity $\lambda > 0$ (for details on the Poisson process see also Section 2.3.1 of Chapter 2). The corresponding default model was developed by Jarrow and Turnbull (1995). Under this model the probability of surviving from time 0 to time t is given by

$$P_{\text{Surv}}^{\text{HP}}(t) = \exp(-\lambda t), \tag{5.2}$$

which corresponds to an expected time of default $\tau = 1/\lambda$.

The probability equals the probability that the counting process – in this case a homogeneous Poisson process $N = \{N_t, t \geq 0\}$ with intensity parameter λ – has not jumped (and hence the company has not defaulted) up to time t:

$$\mathbb{P}(N_t = 0) = \exp(-\lambda t).$$

For example, at a constant default intensity of $\lambda = 0.1$, the probability of default in 5 years is around 9.52%, and the expected time of default is approximatively 10 years. Figure 5.1 shows the evolution of the survival and default probabilities in this case.

Inhomogeneous Case.   Since it is natural to assume that the default intensity varies over time, some generalizations of the Jarrow–Turnbull allow the default intensities to be a deterministic function of time, $\lambda = \{\lambda_t, 0 \leq t \leq T\}$, leading to the so-called

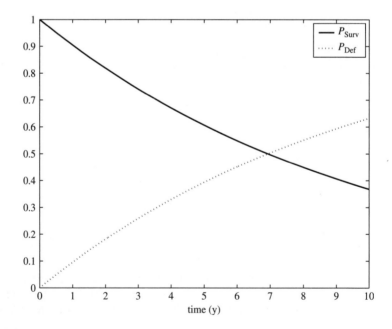

Figure 5.1   Evolution of the survival (solid line) and default (dotted line) probabilities for the Poisson model with constant default intensity of $\lambda = 0.1$

inhomogeneous Poisson (IHP) process. The probability of survive from time 0 to time t is given by:

$$P_{\text{Surv}}^{\text{IHP}}(t) = \exp\left(-\int_0^t \lambda_s \, ds\right). \tag{5.3}$$

As a special case we consider a piecewise constant default intensity:

$$\lambda_t = K_j, \quad T_{j-1} \le t < T_j, \, j = 1, 2, \ldots, 5. \tag{5.4}$$

In this case we have that the survival probability is:

$$P_{\text{Surv}}^{\text{IHP}}(t) = \begin{cases} \exp\left(-K_1 t\right) & 0 \le t < T_1 \\ \exp\left(-K_1 T_1 - K_2(t - T_1)\right) & T_1 \le t < T_2 \\ \exp\left(-K_1 T_1 - K_2(T_2 - T_1) - K_3(t - T_2)\right) & T_2 \le t < T_3 \\ \exp\left(-\sum_{j=1}^{3} K_j(T_j - T_{j-1}) - K_4(t - T_3)\right) & T_3 \le t < T_4 \\ \exp\left(-\sum_{j=1}^{4} K_j(T_j - T_{j-1}) - K_5(t - T_4)\right) & T_4 \le t \le T_5 \end{cases} \tag{5.5}$$

where we have set $T_0 = 0$ for notational convenience.

Figure 5.2 shows the behaviour of the survival and default probabilities for an inhomogeneous Poisson model. In particular, we consider a time horizon of $T = 10$ years and a piecewise constant default intensity of the form (5.5) with the following parameters:

$$\begin{aligned} T_1 &= 1 \text{ year} & K_1 &= 0.02 \\ T_2 &= 3 \text{ years} & K_2 &= 0.05 \\ T_3 &= 5 \text{ years} & K_3 &= 0.07 \\ T_4 &= 7 \text{ years} & K_4 &= 0.10 \\ T_5 &= 10 \text{ years} & K_5 &= 0.13. \end{aligned} \tag{5.6}$$

This model is also often used to extract default probabilities out of a given CDS curve. The idea is simple: assume that we have data for n maturities T_i, $i = 1, \ldots, n$. At these maturities one allows the model to switch to a new level K_i:

$$\lambda_t = K_j, \quad T_{j-1} \le t < T_j, \quad j = 1, 2, \ldots, n. \tag{5.7}$$

Actually one then has as many parameters in the model as data point on the CDS curve and is able to exactly fit the market data by a so-called bootstrapping

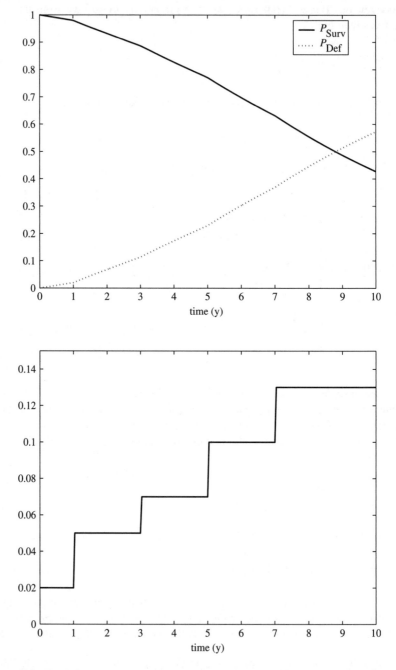

Figure 5.2 Evolution of the survival (solid line) and default (dotted line) probabilities (top plot) for the inhomogeneous Poisson model with piecewise constant default intensity of Equation (5.6). The corresponding default intensity dynamics is shown in the bottom plot

procedure. Out of the CDS spread of the first maturity one calculates K_1. Then one fixes this and considers the CDS curve up to the second maturity. One then looks for the K_2 that can also match the CDS spread at the second maturity (the first maturity is already fitted). Once this K_2 is found, one moves on to the next maturity and so on until the last maturity.

5.1.2 Cox Models

Considering a deterministic intensity implies that the only flow of information available and relevant for default risk is the survival to date (Duffie and Singleton 2003). In order to consider that different information on the creditworthiness of the reference entity will be accessible as time passes, various approaches have been developed that, for instance, link the value of the intensity to other state variables.

In general, a well-accepted approach is to allow for stochastic default intensities $\lambda = \{\lambda_t, 0 \leq t \leq T\}$, intuitively meaning that there is uncertainty about future stress periods of the reference entity. These models are often referred to as *doubly stochastic* to indicate that there are two sources of randomness. On one hand, we have the stochastic behaviour of the default intensity $\lambda = \{\lambda_t, 0 \leq t \leq T\}$. On the other hand, conditional on the process $\lambda = \{\lambda_t, 0 \leq t \leq T\}$, we have the inhomogeneous Poisson process with intensity λ, describing the arrival of default. When dealing with stochastic default intensities, the corresponding counting processes are called Cox-processes. Duffie and Singleton (1999) developed the theory of basic affine intensities, which not only cover, for instance, the case of the Cox–Ingersoll–Ross (CIR) model (Cox *et al.* 1985) but also allow for jumps in the hazard dynamics. Affine processes and their applications in finance are exhaustively covered by Duffie *et al.* (2003). A non-technical summary is included in Duffie and Singleton (2003).

Under these hypotheses, the survival probability up to time t is given by:

$$P_{\text{Surv}}^{\text{DS}}(t) = \mathbb{P}(\tau > t) = \mathbb{E}\left[\exp\left(-\int_0^t \lambda_s \, ds\right)\right].$$

This expression can be obtained by using the property of the iterated expectation (or tower rule), by conditioning on the $\{\lambda_t, 0 \leq t \leq T\}$ process and noting that, if one knows the realization of this intensity process, one is actually working under the above described inhomogeneous Poisson model for which formula (5.3) holds.

As an example of a Cox model driven by a diffusion process, we consider the following, based on CIR dynamics (Cox *et al.* 1985). Assume that the default intensity $\lambda = \{\lambda_t, 0 \leq t \leq T\}$ is described by the following stochastic differential equation:

$$d\lambda_t = \kappa(\eta - \lambda_t) \, dt + \vartheta\sqrt{\lambda_t} \, dW_t, \quad \lambda_0 > 0$$

where $W = \{W_t, 0 \leq t \leq T\}$ is a standard Brownian motion, η is the long-run level, κ is the rate of mean reversion, and ϑ governs the volatility of intensity process.

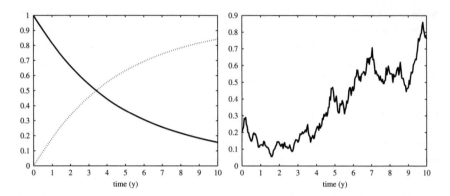

Figure 5.3 Left plot: survival (solid line) and default (dotted line) probabilities for a CIR model with parameterization ($\kappa = 0.1$, $\eta = 0.3$, $\vartheta = 0.2$, $\lambda_0 = 0.02$). Right plot: corresponding CIR process

Under this model, the survival probability up to time t is given by:

$$P_{\text{Surv}}^{\text{CIR}}(t) = \phi_{\text{CIR}}(\mathrm{i}, t; \kappa, \eta, \vartheta, \lambda_0) \tag{5.8}$$

$$= \frac{\exp(\kappa^2 \eta t/\vartheta^2)\exp(-2\lambda_0/(\kappa + \gamma \, \coth(\gamma t/2)))}{(\coth(\gamma t/2) + \kappa \, \sinh(\gamma t/2)/\gamma)^{2\kappa\eta/\vartheta^2}},$$

where $\gamma = \sqrt{\kappa^2 + 2\lambda^2}$.

This expression for the survival probability is linked to the fact that $P_{\text{Surv}}(t)$ can be expressed in terms of the characteristic function of the integrated process (see Chapter 2), as also discussed in Section 5.2:

$$\Lambda_t = \int_0^t \lambda_s \, \mathrm{d}s.$$

A closed-form expression for the characteristic function of the CIR integrated process is given by Cox *et al.*, (1985):

$$\phi_{\text{CIR}}(u, t; \kappa, \eta, \vartheta, \lambda_0) = \frac{\exp(\kappa^2 \eta t/\vartheta^2)\exp(2\lambda_0 \mathrm{i}u/(\kappa + \gamma \, \coth(\gamma t/2)))}{(\coth(\gamma t/2) + \kappa \, \sinh(\gamma t/2)/\gamma)^{2\kappa\eta/\vartheta^2}},$$

where $\gamma = \sqrt{\kappa^2 - 2\lambda^2 \mathrm{i}u}$.

Figure 5.3 (left plot) shows the behaviour of the survival (solid line) and default (dotted line) probabilities under a CIR model; the right plot presents the corresponding CIR process.

5.2   THE INTENSITY-OU MODEL

Consider a reduced-form model with intensity of default $\lambda = \{\lambda_t, 0 \leq t \leq T\}$. Assume that λ follows a Gamma-OU or an IG-OU process, as described in

Section 2.4 of Chapter 2. Hence, the intensity process is modelled by the stochastic differential equation:

$$d\lambda_t = -\vartheta \lambda_t \, dt + dz_{\vartheta t}, \quad \lambda_0 > 0,$$

where ϑ is the arbitrary positive rate parameter and $z = \{z_t, 0 \leq t \leq T\}$ is the Background Driving Lévy Process (BDLP), which we assume to be a non-decreasing Lévy process in order to force the intensity process to be positive. Note that the Gamma-OU case can be rephrased as a special case of the basic affine model introduced by Duffie and Singleton (1999):

$$d\lambda_t = \vartheta(\kappa - \lambda_t)dt + \sigma\sqrt{\lambda_t} \, dW_t + \Delta J_t,$$

where $W = \{W_t, 0 \leq t \leq T\}$ is a standard Brownian motion, and ΔJ_t denotes any jump of a pure jump process $J = \{J_t, 0 \leq t \leq T\}$ occurring at time t. $J = \{J_t, 0 \leq t \leq T\}$ is independent of $W = \{W_t, 0 \leq t \leq T\}$ and has jump sizes independent and exponentially distributed with mean μ and arrival rate $l\vartheta$. The Gamma-OU process can be reformulated under this notation by setting $\sigma = 0, \kappa = 0, l = a$ and $\mu = 1/b$.

The time of default τ is defined as the first jump of the jump process $N = \{N_t, 0 \leq t \leq T\}$ with intensity of default $\lambda = \{\lambda_t, 0 \leq t \leq T\}$:

$$\tau = \inf\{t \in \mathbb{R}^+ | N_t > 0\}.$$

The implied survival probability from 0 to t is given by:

$$P_{\text{Surv}}^{\text{OU}}(t) = \mathbb{P}(\tau > t)$$

$$= \mathbb{E}\left[\exp\left(-\int_0^t \lambda_s ds\right)\right] \tag{5.9}$$

$$= \mathbb{E}\left[\exp\left(-Y_t\right)\right],$$

where $Y_t = \int_0^t \lambda_s ds$ is the intOU process introduced in Chapter 2.

For the Gamma-OU and the IG-OU dynamics, using Equations (2.17) and (2.20), we obtain the following closed-form solutions for the survival probabilities:

$$P_{\text{Surv}}^{\text{Gamma-OU}}(t) = \mathbb{E}\left[\exp\left(-\int_0^t \lambda_s \, ds\right)\right]$$

$$= \phi_{\text{Gamma-OU}}(i, t; \vartheta, a, b, \lambda_0)$$

$$= \exp\left(\frac{-y_0}{\vartheta}(1 - e^{-\vartheta t}) - \frac{\vartheta a}{1 + \vartheta b}\right.$$

$$\left. \times \left(b \log\left(\frac{b}{b + \vartheta^{-1}(1 - e^{-\vartheta t})}\right) + t\right)\right), \tag{5.10}$$

$$P_{\text{Surv}}^{\text{IG-OU}}(t) = \mathbb{E}\left[\exp\left(-\int_0^t \lambda_s \, ds\right)\right]$$

$$= \phi_{\text{IG-OU}}(i, t; \vartheta, a, b, \lambda_0)$$

$$= \exp\left[\frac{-y_0}{\lambda}(1 - \exp(-\lambda t)) - \frac{2a}{b\lambda}A(i, t)\right], \qquad (5.11)$$

where the function A is given by Equation (2.20).

For the Gamma-OU model, we note that the ratio a/b is the average jump size of the compound Poisson process of the BDLP. Moreover, the parameter a is related to the frequency of the jumps of the BDLP: the higher a, the more frequent the jumps. Increasing the average jump size and frequency results in a decrease in the survival probabilities.

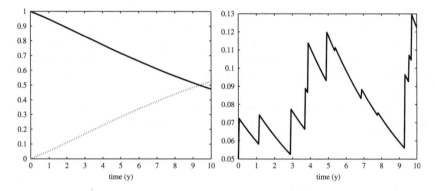

Figure 5.4 Left plot: survival (solid line) and default (dotted line) probabilities for the Gamma-OU model with parameterization ($\vartheta = 0.2, a = 5, b = 50, \lambda_0 = 0.05$). Right plot: corresponding Gamma-OU processes

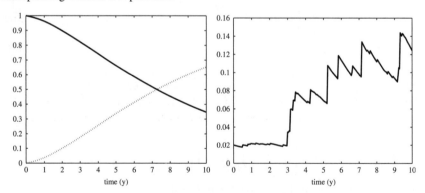

Figure 5.5 Left plot: survival (solid line) and default (dotted line) probabilities for the IG-OU model with ($\vartheta = 0.3, a = 0.8, b = 5, \lambda_0 = 0.02$). Right plot: corresponding IG-OU processes

For the IG-OU model, the dynamics is a bit more involved since the BDLP is a sum of two processes (see Section 2.4.2 of Chapter 2).

In Figures 5.4 and 5.5 we calculate default and survival probabilities under the Gamma-OU model and the IG-OU model respectively (left plots); we also plot a realization of the intensity process under the respective models (right plots).

5.3   CALIBRATION OF THE MODEL ON CDS TERM STRUCTURES

Under the Gamma-OU and IG-OU dynamics it is possible to estimate the CDS par spread of Equation (4.3)

$$c^{T-\text{CDS}} = \frac{(1 - R) \sum_{i=1}^{n} D(0, t_i)(P_{\text{Surv}}(t_{i-1}) - P_{\text{Surv}}(t_i))}{\sum_{i=1}^{n} D(0, t_i) P_{\text{Surv}}(t_i) \Delta t_i}.$$

using Equations (5.10) and (5.11) for the survival probabilities. We calibrate our intensity-OU models to the CDS term structures of the iTraxx Europe Index, as described in Section 3.1.2. Each term structure includes prices of CDSs for five different times to maturity (respectively $T_1 = 1$, $T_2 = 3$, $T_3 = 5$, $T_4 = 7$, and $T_5 = 10$ years). In our exercise, we set for convenience $T_0 = 0$. For each component the database includes the complete weekly time series from 5 January 2005 to 8 February 2006. In the calibrations the discounting factor $D = \{D(0, t), 0 \leq t \leq T\}$ is taken from the (bond) market on the corresponding day. The recovery rate for all the iTraxx Europe Index assets is fixed at $R = 40\%$. The Central Processing Unit time required to calibrate our OU-model to *all* the 125 CDS term structures together for a given point in time (i.e. for a given week) is around 1 minute.

For comparison purposes, the capabilities of the OU model are tested by calibrating on the same term structures the following models:

(1) the homogeneous Poisson (HP) model (Jarrow and Turnbull 1995), see Equation (5.2);
(2) the inhomogeneous Poisson (IHP) model with piecewise constant default intensity, see Equations (5.4) and (5.5);
(3) the Cox–Ingersoll–Ross (CIR) model (Cox *et al.* 1985), see Equation (5.8).

To discuss the outcomes, we concentrate on two companies of the iTraxx, *Zurich Insurance* and *Continental*, and in Table 5.1 on page 98 present the calibration results matching market data as of 21 July 2005. Market CDS prices are compared with the prices obtained using the models. For each calibration the RMSE values are also given. Figures 5.6 and 5.7 visualize the calibrated term structures (top plots) and the default probabilities as a function of time (bottom plots) for the five models. Market data are represented by the circles.

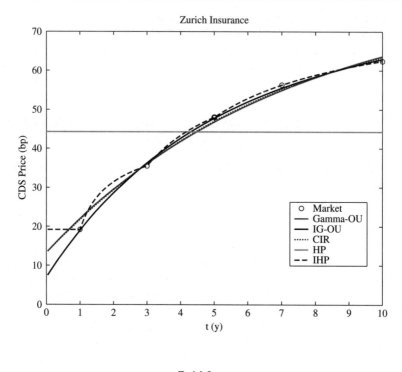

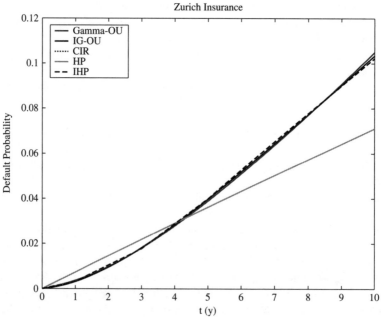

Figure 5.6 Term structures (top plot) and default probabilities (bottom plots) for *Zurich Insurance* for the five models

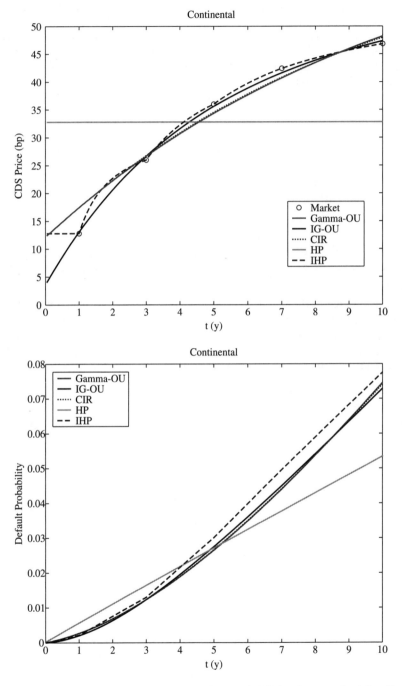

Figure 5.7 Term structures (top plot) and default probabilities (bottom plots) for *Continental* for the five models

Table 5.1 Examples of calibrated CDS term structures versus market data (in bp), with corresponding RMSE values

Company		1 y	3 y	5 y	7 y	10 y	RSME
Zurich	Market	19	35	48	56	62	
Insurance	HP	44	44	44	44	44	15.43
	IHP	19	35	48	56	62	–
	CIR	22	36	47	55	63	1.61
	GOU	22	36	47	55	64	1.79
	IG-OU	19	36	48	55	63	0.77
Continental	Market	13	26	36	42	47	
	HP	33	33	33	33	33	12.12
	IHP	13	26	36	42	47	–
	CIR	17	27	35	41	48	2.00
	GOU	17	27	34	41	48	2.14
	IG-OU	13	27	36	42	47	0.45

Results highlight the complete failure of the HP model to match market data. Concerning the IHP case, the model can match perfectly the market quotes; however, the behaviour of the term structure between two subsequent time horizons is often rather doubtful, due to the piecewise constant assumption. The CIR, Gamma-OU and IG-OU models can all be nicely calibrated to market data.

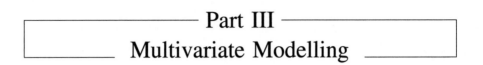

Part III
Multivariate Modelling

6
Multivariate Credit Products

Credit markets have seen an explosive growth over the last decade. New multivariate products, like CDOs, CDO^2, CCPIs, CPDOs, have been brought to the market and some of them have an unprecedented complexity. In this chapter we give an overview of the most popular multivariate credit derivatives, like credit indices and CDO structures. In Chapter 9 we go into detail for the more exotic products.

In the modelling of multivariate products, i.e. products that depend on several underliers, the dependency among the underlying instruments is of crucial importance. However, as always, a balance needs to be maintained between sophistication and tractability. Often, therefore, one is looking for quite simple dependency structures (even often summarized in only one number – correlation). It needs to be said that clearly the world is much more complex and extreme care must be taken in the blind belief of such simplistic models.

6.1 CDOs

In this section we describe so-called (Synthetic) Collateralized Credit Obligations (CDOs). These products are complex multivariate credit risk derivatives. Essentially, a CDO transfers the credit risk of a reference portfolio of assets in a tranched way. Losses are applied in reverse order of seniority. Hence losses will first affect the lowest tranche (often referred to as the *equity tranche*), next the so-called *mezzanine tranches*, and finally *the senior tranches*. Figure 6.1 shows schematically how a CDO is built. Each tranche is defined in terms of upper and lower points representing the percentage of the total notional covered by the tranche itself. The lower point is usually referred to as the *attachment point* while the upper one is known as the *detachment point*. For instance for the mezzanine tranche in Figure 6.1 the attachment and detachment points are 6% and 9% respectively. Each tranche receives a periodic payment (the swap premium). Clearly, lower tranches offer higher coupons (spreads) to compensate for the added default risk.

The first CDO was issued in 1987 by bankers at now-defunct Drexel Burnham Lambert Inc. for Imperial Savings Association, a savings institution that later became insolvent and was taken over by the Resolution Trust Corporation.

Cash CDOs involve a portfolio of cash assets, such as loans, corporate bonds, asset-backed securities or mortgage-backed securities. Ownership of the assets is transferred to a legal entity (known as a special purpose vehicle, or SPV) issuing the CDO's tranches. Synthetic CDOs holders do not own cash assets like bonds or loans. Instead, synthetic CDOs holders gain credit exposure to a portfolio of fixed income assets without owning those assets through the use of CDSs. Hybrid CDOs are an intermediate instrument between cash CDOs and synthetic CDOs.

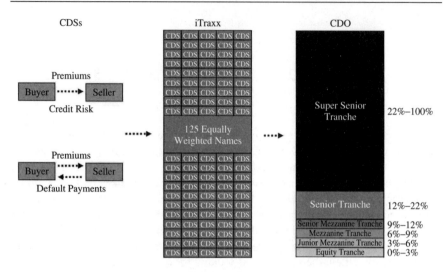

Figure 6.1   CDO mechanisme and CDO tranches

There exist some standardized synthetic CDOs: the most popular ones are the CDOs based on the portfolio of CDSs in the iTraxx Europe Main index and the Dow Jones CDX.NA.IG index. The tranches points are 3, 6, 9, 12 and 22% for the former and 3, 7, 10, 15 and 30% for the latter. So, unlike 'bespoke' tranches, index tranches have standardized documentation and use standard attachment and detachment points. Index tranches are quoted on all the maturities of the indices, which are 3, 5, 7 and 10 years.

A CDO tranche is typically quoted with an upfront and a running spread. The upfront is the percentage of the notional that one receives upfront (i.e. when the deal is struck) if one sells protection: the running spread is the yearly spread that one (additionally) receives during the lifetime of the tranche. It often turns out that upfront is agreed to be zero for most tranches. This is the case for the standardized iTraxx and CDX CDOs; for these very popular CDOs only the [0–3%] tranche has an upfront until end of 2008. Since beginning of 2009, the CDX [3%–7%] tranche has also an upfront. For all these tranches, for the moment the running spread is fixed at 500 bp and it is the upfront (in percentage points) that is quoted and fluctuates over time.

For example, the situation on 16 October 2008 for the iTraxx Europe Main tranches (Series 10) for the 5-year structure is given in Table 6.1; the situation for the Dow Jones CDX NA IG is summarized in Table 6.2.

In order to understand the CDO mechanism, it is sometimes useful to think about it as a bath that can be filled with water. Imagine that we have a CDO of 125 companies and that, in the case of default, each company has a recovery, R of say 40%. Then each default among the 125 companies fills the '100 litre bath' with $100 \times (1 - R)/125 = 0.48$ litres of water. If you have sold protection on a certain tranche, you receive a fee on the amount of your tranche that is not under water.

Table 6.1 iTraxx Europe Main (5-year) Tranches on 16 October 2008 (Series 10)

Tranche	Upfront (%)	Running spread (bps)
[0%–3%]	59.57	500
[3%–6%]	0	1086.58
[6%–9%]	0	576.66
[9%–12%]	0	288.12
[12%–22%]	0	115.99
[22%–100%]	0	41.89

Table 6.2 Dow Jones CDX.NA.IG (5-year) Tranches on 16 October 2008 (Series 11)

Tranche	Upfront (%)	Running spread (bps)
[0%–3%]	73.12	500
[3%–7%]	0	1389.20
[7%–10%]	0	740.80
[10%–15%]	0	330.60
[15%–30%]	0	80.80
[30%–100%]	0	51.10

So if the [3%–6%] tranche is quoted 1086.58 bps on a 5-year CDO and you decide to sell protection for 100m EUR, you receive per year 10.8658m EUR for 5 years or until the 7th default in the list of 125 companies. Indeed, if each default adds 0.48 litres of water, then your tranche is coming partially under water after the 7th default. The bath is then filled up to $7 \times 0.48 = 3.36$ litres and your tranche starts at the 3-litre level. If the 7th default occurs, you have to pay out $100 \times 0.36/3 = 12$m EUR, because 0.36 litre of your total 3-litre-thick tranche is under water, meaning, that 12% is now under water. From then on you receive a premium of only $0.88 \times 10.8658 = 9.5620$m EUR per year because only 88% of the tranche is still above water. For each other default you have to pay out an additional 16m EUR ($100m \times 0.48/3$) and your yearly fee payment is reduced by $0.16 \times 10.8658 = 1.7385$m EUR. You do this until maturity or until the 13th default. Immediately before the 13th default your tranche is filled up to the $12 \times 0.48 = 5.76$-litre level. With the 13th default the full tranche is now under water and for the final part you have to pay $100 \times 0.24/3 = 8$m EUR. All your 100m EUR has then been spent. Your maximum profit over 5 years (ignoring discount factors) is 54.329m EUR (if there were only 6 defaults or less). Your maximum loss over 5 years is 100m EUR (if there are 13 or more defaults). To be fully correct we also have to note that, in the case of a default, the super-senior tranche is reduced in size with a recovery value ($100 \times R/125 = 0.32$ litres of water) and that, after a default, a spread is no longer received on that part.

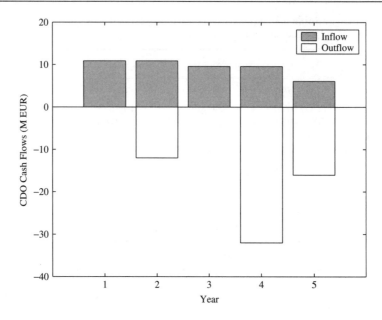

Figure 6.2   Example of 5-year CDO cash flows for the protection seller of the [3%–6%] tranche

The timing of the defaults are, of course, also very important. Let us focus on the previous example of a 5-year CDO and take again the [3%–6%] tranche. Hypothesize that we have six defaults during the first year: one just at the end of the second year, none in the third year, two at the end of the fourth year, and one just before the CDO expires in year 5. We note that the example is constructed in such a way that no accrued payments are needed. The cash flows for the protection seller (see also Figure 6.2) are as follows:

- For the first year, the protection seller will receive the complete yearly fee of 10.8658m EUR and will pay out zero, since no loss will affect the tranche.
- For the second year, the protection seller will receive the complete yearly fee of 10.8658m EUR and pay out 12m EUR at the end of the year when the 7th default occurred and the tranche is hit for the first time.
- For the third year, the protection seller will receive a lower yearly fee of 9.5620m EUR and pay out zero, since no additional defaults affect the tranche.
- For the fourth year, the protection seller will receive the same fee as the year before of 9.5620m EUR and pay out 32m EUR at the end of that year, since at that time two more defaults occur.
- For the fifth year, the protection seller will receive a decreased fee of 6.085m EUR and pay out 16m EUR just before expiry, since one more default occurs.

Pricing a CDO tranche is very similar to pricing a CDS. In case of a zero upfront it comes down to looking for the fair spread s^{CDO}, such that the present expected value of the premium leg equals the present expected value of the loss (default) leg. The present expected value of the premium leg equals

$$\text{PV}_{\text{Fee}}^{\text{CDO}} = s^{\text{CDO}} \sum_{i=1}^{n} N(1 - \mathbb{E}[L_i^{\text{Tr}}])D(0, t_i)\Delta t_i,$$

where t_i, $i = 1, \ldots, n$, are the payment dates, Δt_i is the year fraction, N is the notional, $D(0, t_i)$ is the discounting factor, and L_i^{Tr} is the loss of the tranche at time t_i. Similarly,

$$\text{PV}_{\text{Loss}}^{\text{CDO}} = \sum_{i=1}^{n} N(\mathbb{E}[L_i^{\text{Tr}}] - \mathbb{E}[L_{i-1}^{\text{Tr}}])D(0, t_i).$$

Hence

$$s^{\text{CDO}} = \frac{\sum_{i=1}^{n}(\mathbb{E}[L_i^{\text{Tr}}] - \mathbb{E}[L_{i-1}^{\text{Tr}}])D(0, t_i)}{\sum_{i=1}^{n}(1 - \mathbb{E}[L_i^{\text{Tr}}])D(0, t_i)\Delta t_i}, \tag{6.1}$$

balances the PV of fee and loss legs.

In the case of an upfront with a fixed spread, s^* (typically 500 bps) one looks for Upf, the upfront, such that the PV of the fee (the left-hand side of the equation below) equals the PV of the losses (the right-hand side)

$$\text{Upf} \times N + s^* \sum_{i=1}^{n} N(1 - \mathbb{E}[L_i^{\text{Tr}}])D(0, t_i)\Delta t_i = \sum_{i=1}^{n} N(\mathbb{E}[L_i^{\text{Tr}}]$$
$$- \mathbb{E}[L_{i-1}^{\text{Tr}}])D(0, t_i)$$

or equivalently

$$\text{Upf} = \sum_{i=1}^{n}(\mathbb{E}[L_i^{\text{Tr}}] - \mathbb{E}[L_{i-1}^{\text{Tr}}])D(0, t_i) - s^* \sum_{i=1}^{n}(1 - \mathbb{E}[L_i^{\text{Tr}}])D(0, t_i)\Delta t_i.$$

We note that, as in the CDS case, to be fully accurate the accrual on default also needs to be taken into account. Further, if we deal with the super-senior tranche, the reduction in size by recovery values of defaults in the portfolio also needs to be taken into account in the above formulas (however the effect of this is rather small.)

6.2   CREDIT INDICES

A credit index swap is one of the most liquid portfolio derivatives. A position in such a credit index can be seen as a CDO [0%–100%] tranche position. By taking a position in the index, one actually takes a position in all the constituents. Investors can be long or short the index, which is equivalent to being protection sellers or buyers. Credit default swap indices are often completely standardized and may therefore be more liquid and traded at a smaller bid–offer spread. Therefore, they allow an investor to transfer credit risk in a more efficient manner than using groups of single CDSs. This is one of the main reasons why index positions are often used to hedge credit risk. Moreover, the introduction of liquid and easily tradable CDS indices opened the door for a new generation of credit derivatives products based on these indices (CPPIs, CPDOs, ...).

There are currently two main families of CDS indices: CDX and iTraxx. CDX indices contain North American and Emerging Market companies and iTraxx contain companies from the rest of the world. The constituents of the indices are changed every six months – a process known as 'rolling' the index. The roll dates are 20 March and 20 September each year.

The most popular CDS indices are, at present:

- The Europe Benchmark Index *iTraxx Europe Main*, containing the 125 most actively European traded names in the six months prior to the index roll.
- The *iTraxx Europe HiVol*, which contains the 30 highest spread (riskiest) names from the iTraxx Europe index.
- The *iTraxx Europe Crossover*, containing 50 subinvestment European grade names.
- The *Dow Jones CDX.NA.IG*, containing 125 North American investment grade CDSs.
- The *Dow Jones CDX.NA.HY*, containing 100 North American high-yield CDSs.

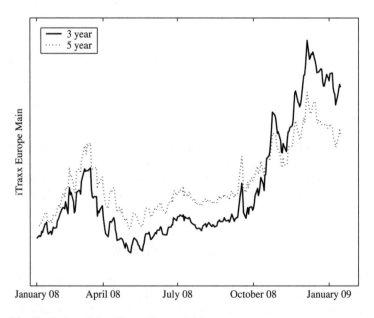

Figure 6.3 Evolution of the iTraxx Europe Main

- The *Dow Jones CDX.NA.IG.HiVol*, which contains the 30 highest spread (riskiest) names from the Dow Jones CDX.NA.IG index.
- The *Dow Jones CDX.NA.XO*, containing 35 North American high-yield/ investment grade CDSs.

Each index has typically a value (often close to the average value of the underlying CDSs) for several terms (3, 5, 7, 10 years). The 5- and 7-year indices are in most cases the most liquid ones.

In Figure 6.3, one sees the evolution of the iTraxx Europe Main (3 and 5 years) over a period of 1 year, from January 2008 to January 2009. One clearly sees the credit crunch crises in autumn 2008.

7
Collateralized Debt Obligations

7.1 INTRODUCTION

The advent of standard Collateralized Debt Obligation (CDO) tranches on the standard CDS index as the reference portfolio has greatly enhanced liquidity and transparency in the synthetic CDO market. Nowadays, we observe daily pricing on a range of tranches linked to US, European and Asian investment grades and high-yield CDS indices.

The price of a CDO tranche is a function of many things: the probability of default of the underlying of the CDSs in the reference portfolio, their recovery values in case of default, the current interest rate environment and, most importantly, the default dependency (correlation) between the assets in the reference portfolio. Actually, since the introduction of the one-factor Gaussian copula model (also known as the one-factor Normal model) for pricing synthetic CDO tranches, correlation is seen as an exogenous parameter used to match observed market quotes. Therefore, a CDO position can also be seen as a correlation trade: an equity tranche investor can be shown to be long the default correlation between the credits in the underlying CDS index while a senior tranche investor is short this default correlation. Taken into account that the senior tranche is often rated as AAA quality, selling protection on this tranche could be seen as being short default correlation. The credit crunch, which led to a tremendous increase of the default correlation, has therefore hurt many AAA investors.

Initially, the market focused on compound correlation as the standard convention. In tandem with the concept of volatility in the Black–Scholes option-pricing framework, compound correlation was the parameter to be put in the model to match observed market prices of tranches (see, for instance, O'Kane and Livasey 2004). Under this approach each tranche was priced by a correlation coefficient independent from those of the other tranches and depending on the attachment and detachment points. As also discussed in Garcia and Goossens (2007a), the compound correlation approach presents several problems such as the fact that it cannot be extended to pricing of tranches with non-standard points (such as, for example, [5%–8%]). Moreover, during some market events non-meaningful values may be found for implied compound correlation – for example, during the auto crisis of May 2005. The current widespread market approach is to use the concept of *Base Correlation* (BC), first introduced by McGinty *et al.* (2004). In the base correlation methodology only base tranches, i.e. tranches with an attachment point 0, are used. The price of a tranche $[K_1 - K_2]$ is calculated using the two base tranches with K_1 and K_2 as detachment points (see Figure 7.1).

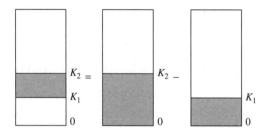

Figure 7.1 Base correlation approach: each tranche is treated as the difference between two base tranches

Using BC, it is quite straightforward to bootstrap between standard attachment points, as detailed in Section 7.5. Additionally, the BC concept is quite adapted to interpolation for non-standard tranches. Hence the [5%–8%] tranche would be priced by interpolating the BC curve for values at 5% and 8% respectively. The methodology, however, has some weaknesses. First, it is very sensitive to the interpolation technique used. Even worse, the methodology may not be arbitrage-free. Finally, the methodology does not provide any guidance on how to extrapolate the curve, especially below the 3% attachment point. Some of these problems have been addressed in Garcia and Goossens (2007a) – see also Garcia and Goossens (2007b).

In this chapter we discuss how to model and price CDO tranches. Then, we elaborate on Lévy BC. Lévy BC is actually a straightforward generalization of the classical Gaussian BC. It differs only in the underlying one-factor model. We make a comparison of several Lévy models with the classical Gaussian case.

The remainder of this chapter is organized as follows. First we introduce the one-factor Normal model and discuss how to model and price CDO tranches. Next, in Section 7.3, we review the generic one-factor Lévy model for the valuation of CDO tranches. Then, we discuss the concept of a Lévy base correlation and compare hedge parameters under the different models in Section 7.6. We focus on the deltas of the tranches with respect to the index.

This chapter is mainly based on Albrecher *et al.* (2007), Garcia *et al.* (2008) and Masol and Schoutens (2007). Related literature is Baxter (2007), Guégan and Houdain (2005), Hooda (2006), Kalemanova *et al.* (2007) and Moosbrucker (2006).

7.2 THE GAUSSIAN ONE-FACTOR MODEL

We model over a finite horizon T a portfolio of n obligors such that they all have equal weights in the portfolio. For simplicity, we will assume that each obligor i, $i \in \{1, 2, \ldots, n\}$, has the same recovery rate R in case of default. One can generalize the arguments below to a general situation, but for the sake of explanation, we take equal weights with R the same for each obligor.

We assume also that we know for each obligor the individual default probability term structure $p_i(t)$, $0 \le t \le T$, which is the probability that obligor i will default before time t. This term structure can be extracted out of a CDS curve, as explained in Section 5.1.

The Gaussian one-factor model describes the 'healthiness' of an obligor by a latent variable:

$$A_i = \sqrt{\rho}\, Y + \sqrt{1 - \rho}\, \varepsilon_i, \qquad i = 1, \dots, n; \tag{7.1}$$

where Y and ε_i, $i = 1, \dots, n$, are i.i.d. standard Normal distributed. Note that each A_i, is again standard Normal distributed and hence $\mathbb{E}[A_i] = 0$ and $\mathrm{Var}[A_i] = 1$.

Actually this model assumes that the vector of n latent variables A_i is multivariate standard Normal distributed and this is the reason one often refers to it as the 'Gaussian Copula Model'. The correlation matrix is of a very simple form: it is 1 on the diagonal and ρ elsewhere, since we have for $i \neq j$

$$\mathrm{Corr}[A_i, A_j] = \frac{\mathbb{E}[A_i A_j] - \mathbb{E}[A_i]\mathbb{E}[A_j]}{\sqrt{\mathrm{Var}[A_i]}\sqrt{\mathrm{Var}[A_j]}} = \mathbb{E}[A_i A_j] = \mathbb{E}[(\sqrt{\rho}\, Y)^2] = \rho.$$

We say that the ith obligor *defaults at time* t if the latent value A_i falls below some preset barrier $K_i(t)$: $A_i \leq K_i(t)$. In order to match default probabilities under this model with default probabilities $p_i(t)$ observed in the market, we have to set $K_i(t) := \Phi^{[-1]}(p_i(t))$, where Φ is the cumulative distribution function of the standard Normal distribution. Indeed, then

$$\mathbb{P}(A_i \leq K_i(t)) = \mathbb{P}(A_i \leq \Phi^{[-1]}(p_i(t))) = \Phi(\Phi^{[-1]}(p_i(t))) = p_i(t).$$

Note that, the default time $\tau^{(i)}$ of the ith obligor then equals:

$$\tau^{(i)} = p_i^{[-1]}\big(\Phi(A_i)\big).$$

The one-factor Gaussian copula model has been very popular and is extensively used by market participants, often in combination with the so-called *recursion algorithm* which was first introduced by Andersen *et al.* (2003). This recursive algorithm allows us to compute very efficiently the probability to have a number of defaults in a group of n firms. We will give the details of this technique after having set up the generic one-factor Lévy models, because the same technique can be used in this more general framework. The reason we set up an alternative model is because the one-factor Gaussian model does not seem to have a realistic dependency structure. Indeed, under the Gaussian copula it is very unlikely (due to the light tail behaviour of the Normal distribution) that we will see many joint defaults. Hence, because the probability of this is extremely small, senior tranches of the CDO will be underpriced. This is often then compensated by blowing up correlations to artificially high values.

7.3 GENERIC ONE-FACTOR LÉVY MODEL

The idea is to generate standardized (zero mean, variance 1) multivariate random non-normal vectors with a prescribed correlation. In order to do this, we generate

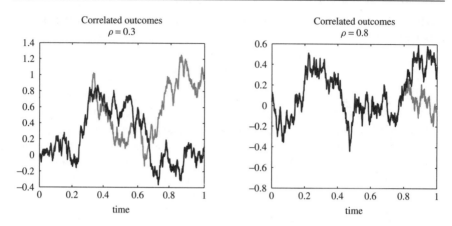

Figure 7.2 Simulation of A_1 and A_2 for two different correlation values

correlation by letting Lévy processes run some time together and then let them run freely (see Figure 7.2 for an example with two obligors).

Indeed, one can write the one-factor Gaussian model 7.1 differently:

$$A_i = W_\rho + W^{(i)}_{1-\rho}, i = 1, \ldots, n;$$

where W and the $W^{(i)}$'s are independent standard Brownian motions. Hence, A_i is the endpoint of the sum of a Brownian motion run for ρ times common to all obligors, and an individual independent Brownian motion for a period of $(1 - \rho)$ times.

Compare this with the following. We will look at the end positions of two children who run for, say, an hour. First, the children have to give a hand to each other for some fraction (ρ) of that hour; after that they run independently from each other (for $(1 - \rho)$ hour). Of course, if they must run together for most of the time (ρ is close to 1), their endpoints will not be very far away from each other; there is a high degree of dependency (high correlation). If they are allowed to run freely from the beginning (ρ is small), their endpoints will be quite independent of each other (low correlation).

The above construction can be completely generalized to the Lévy setting: let $X = \{X_t, 0 \leq t \leq 1\}$ be a Lévy process based on an infinitely divisible distribution L, i.e. X_1 follows the law L. Assume that $\mathbb{E}[X_1] = 0$ and $\text{Var}[X_1] = 1$. Denote by H_t the cumulative distribution function of X_t, $0 \leq t \leq 1$:

$$H_t(x) = \mathbb{P}(X_t \leq x),$$

and assume that it is continuous. It may be shown that $\text{Var}[X_t] = t$. Note that we will only work with Lévy processes with time running over the unit interval. Let $X^{(i)} = \{X^{(i)}_t, t \in [0, 1]\}$, $i = 1, 2, \ldots, n$, and let X denote independent and identically distributed Lévy processes (i.e. all processes are independent of each other and are based on the same infinitely divisible distribution L).

Let $0 < \rho < 1$ be the correlation; the latent variable of firm i is of the form:

$$A_i = X_\rho + X_{1-\rho}^{(i)}, \quad i = 1, \ldots, n.$$

By the stationary and independent increment property of Lévy processes, A_i has the same distribution as X_1, i.e. $A_i \simeq L$. Hence $\mathbb{E}[A_i] = 0$, $\text{Var}[A_i] = 1$. Moreover, one can easily show that the following formula for the correlation holds:

$$\text{Corr}\left[A_i, A_j\right] = \frac{\mathbb{E}\left[A_i A_j\right] - \mathbb{E}[A_i]\mathbb{E}[A_j]}{\sqrt{\text{Var}[A_i]}\sqrt{\text{Var}[A_j]}} = \rho, \quad i \neq j.$$

So, starting from any mother standardized infinitely divisible law, we can set up a one-factor model with the required correlation.

Completely similar to the Gaussian case, the ith obligor defaults at time t if the value A_i falls below some preset barrier $K_i(t)$: $A_i \leq K_i(t)$. In order to match default probabilities under this model with default probabilities $p_i(t)$ observed in the market, set $K_i(t) := H_1^{[-1]}(p_i(t))$.

Further, we have that the default time $\tau^{(i)}$ of the ith obligor equals:

$$\tau^{(i)} = p_i^{[-1]}\big(H_1(A_i)\big).$$

Recursive Loss Algorithm

Let $M_{t,n}$ be the number of defaults in the portfolio (of n obligors) up to time t. We calculate, by the so-called *recursive loss algorithm* (Andersen *et al.* 2003), the probability $P(M_{t,n} = k)$, $k = 0, 1, \ldots, n$, of having k out of n defaults until time t. We have

$$\Pi_n^k(t) := \mathbb{P}(M_{t,n} = k)$$

$$= \int_{-\infty}^{+\infty} \mathbb{P}(M_{t,n} = k | X_\rho = y) \, dH_\rho(y), \quad k = 0, \ldots, n.$$

Denote by $p_i(t; y)$ the probability that the firm's value A_i is below the barrier $K_i(t)$, given that the systematic factor X_ρ takes the value y. Because, conditional on the common factor X_ρ, the default events are independent, we have

$$p_i(t; y) = \mathbb{P}(A_i \leq K_i(t) | X_\rho = y)$$

$$= \mathbb{P}(X_\rho + X_{1-\rho}^{(i)} \leq K_i(t) | X_\rho = y) = H_{1-\rho}(K_i(t) - y).$$

Denote by $\Pi_{m,y}^k(t)$ the conditional probability to have k out of a group of m defaults before time t, given $X_\rho = y$, $k = 0, 1, \ldots, m$. Then $\Pi_{n,y}^k(t)$ can be calculated recursively. We start with $m = 0$ and move on to the next m until $m = n$ by using:

$$\Pi^0_{0,y}(t) \equiv 1;$$

$$\Pi^0_{m,y}(t) = \Pi^0_{m-1,y}(t)\,(1 - p_m(t;\,y));$$

$$\Pi^k_{m,y}(t) = \Pi^k_{m-1,y}(t)\,(1 - p_m(t;\,y))$$
$$\qquad\qquad + \Pi^{k-1}_{m-1,y}(t)\,p_m(t;\,y), \quad k = 1, \ldots, m-1;$$

$$\Pi^m_{m,y}(t) = \Pi^{m-1}_{m-1,y}(t)\,p_m(t;\,y).$$

The first line is the start of the recursive procedure. The third line can be interpreted as follows. To calculate the conditional probability at time t to have k defaults out of a group of m, we look at obligor m and the previous group (of size $(m-1)$). Because we work recursively, we know the probability of having $(k-1)$ or k defaults in this subgroup of size $m-1$. These probabilities are given by $\Pi^{k-1}_{m-1,y}$ and $\Pi^k_{m-1,y}$ respectively. In order to have k defaults in the big group of size m, we can have k defaults in the subgroup of size $(m-1)$ and no default of the mth obligor, or a default of obligor m together with $(k-1)$ defaults in the subgroup. Because of independence (we are working conditionally on the common factor), the first situation happens with probability $\Pi^k_{m-1,y}(t)\,(1 - p_m(t;\,y))$ and the other situation occurs with probability $\Pi^{k-1}_{m-1,y}(t)\,p_m(t;\,y)$. The second and fourth lines are similar but deal with the boundary cases $k = 0$ and $k = m$.

The unconditional probability of exactly k defaults out of n firms is

$$\Pi^k_n(t) := \mathbb{P}(M_{t,n} = k) = \int_{-\infty}^{\infty} \mathbb{P}(M_{t,n} = k | X_\rho = y)\,\mathrm{d}H_\rho(y)$$

$$= \int_{-\infty}^{\infty} \Pi^k_{n,y}(t)\,\mathrm{d}H_\rho(y).$$

The percentage loss $L_{t,n}$ on the portfolio notional at time t is

$$L_{t,n} = \frac{(1-R)M_{t,n}}{n}.$$

Hence, the expected percentage loss $\mathbb{E}[L_{t,n}]$ on the portfolio notional at time t is

$$\mathbb{E}[L_{t,n}] = \frac{(1-R)}{n} \sum_{k=1}^{n} k \cdot \Pi^k_n(t);$$

and the expected percentage loss on the CDO tranche $[K_1\%{-}K_2\%]$ is

$$\mathbb{E}\left[L^{K_1,K_2}_{t,n}\right] = \frac{\mathbb{E}\left[\min\{L_{t,n},\,K_2\}\right] - \mathbb{E}\left[\min\{L_{t,n},\,K_1\}\right]}{K_2 - K_1}.$$

The fair premium for the tranche $[K_1\% - K_2\%]$ can then be calculated, recalling Equation (6.1), as

$$s^{\text{CDO}} = \frac{\sum_j \left\{ \mathbb{E}\left[L_{t_j,n}^{K_1,K_2}\right] - \mathbb{E}\left[L_{t_{j-1},n}^{K_1,K_2}\right] \right\} D(0,t_j)}{\sum_j \left\{ 1 - \mathbb{E}\left[L_{t_j,n}^{K_1,K_2}\right] \right\} (t_j - t_{j-1}) D(0,t_j)},$$

where both summations are taken over the set of payment dates, and $D(0,t)$ is the discount factor from time t to time 0. As for the other instruments (e.g. see Equation (3.2) for the CDS), the quantity in the denominator is referred to as the *risky annuity* and equals the expected present value of 1 bp paid in premium until default or maturity, whichever is sooner.

7.4 EXAMPLES OF LÉVY MODELS

Shifted Gamma

Recall that the characteristic function of the Gamma distribution, Gamma(a,b), $a, b > 0$, is given by

$$\phi_{\text{Gamma}}(u; a, b) = (1 - \mathrm{i}u/b)^{-a}, \quad u \in \mathbb{R}.$$

Let us start with a unit-variance Gamma-process $G = \{G_t, t \geq 0\}$ with parameters $a > 0$ and $b = \sqrt{a}$ such that $\mu := \mathbb{E}[G_1] = \sqrt{a}$, $\text{Var}[G_1] = 1$. As a driving Lévy process, we then take the *Shifted Gamma process*

$$X_t = \mu t - G_t, \quad 0 \leq t \leq 1.$$

The interpretation in terms of latent (firm) value is that there is a deterministic up trend $\sqrt{a}\,t$ and random downward shocks $\{G_t\}$.

The one-factor Shifted Gamma Lévy model is

$$A_i = X_\rho + X_{1-\rho}^{(i)}, \quad i = 1, 2, \ldots, n,$$

where X_ρ and $\{X_{1-\rho}^{(i)}\}_{i=1}^n$ are independent standardized Shifted Gamma processes. Hereafter we will refer to the Shifted Gamma-Lévy model with parameters $a > 0$ and $b = \sqrt{a}$ as *Gamma(a)*.

The unconditional probability of exactly k defaults out of n firms becomes

$$\Pi_n^k(t) = \int_0^{+\infty} \Pi_{n,(\sqrt{a}\,\rho - u/b)}^k(t) \frac{1}{\Gamma(a\rho)} u^{a\rho-1} \exp(-u)\, \mathrm{d}u,$$

where the last integral can be calculated by a different method (e.g. by applying Gauss–Laguerre quadrature); for details we refer to Dobránszky (2008).

Shifted Inverse Gaussian

The Inverse Gaussian IG(a, b) law with parameters $a > 0$ and $b > 0$ has characteristic function

$$\phi_{\text{IG}}(u; a, b) = \exp\left(-a(\sqrt{-2iu + b^2} - b)\right), \quad u \in \mathbb{R}.$$

Here, we start with a unit variance IG process $I = \{I_t, t \geq 0\}$ with parameters $a > 0$ and $b = a^{1/3}$ such that $\mu := \mathbb{E}[I_1] = a^{2/3}$, $\text{Var}[I_1] = 1$. Then, similar to the Gamma case,

$$X_t = \mu t - I_t, \quad t \in [0, 1].$$

The one-factor shifted IG-Lévy model, hereafter referred to as the IG*(a)* model, is

$$A_i = X_\rho + X^{(i)}_{1-\rho},$$

where $X_\rho, \{X^{(i)}_{1-\rho}\}^n_{i=1}$ are independent shifted IG processes. In order to compute the unconditional probabilities $\Pi^k_n(t)$ one can rely on numerical integration schemes using the density of the IG processes or apply Laplace transform inversion methods.

Shifted CMY

The CMY(C, M, Y) distribution with parameters $C > 0$, $M > 0$ and $Y < 1$ has characteristic function

$$\phi_{\text{CMY}}(u; C, M, Y) = \exp\left\{C\Gamma(-Y)\left[(M - iu)^Y - M^Y\right]\right\}, \quad u \in \mathbb{R}.$$

Let us start here again with a CMY process $C = \{C_t, t \geq 0\}$ with parameters $C > 0$, $Y < 1$ and $M = (C\Gamma(2 - Y))^{\frac{1}{2-Y}}$, so that the mean of the process is $\mu := \left(C\Gamma(1 - Y)(1 - Y)^{Y-1}\right)^{\frac{1}{2-Y}}$ and the variance is equal to 1. As the driving Lévy process we take

$$X_t = \mu t - C_t, \quad t \in [0, 1].$$

The one-factor shifted CMY-Lévy model, hereafter referred to as the CMY$(C; Y)$ model, is

$$A_i = X_\rho + X^{(i)}_{1-\rho},$$

where $X_\rho, \{X^{(i)}_{1-\rho}\}^n_{i=1}$ are independent shifted CMY processes.

Since neither the cumulative distribution function $H_{\text{CMY}}(x; C, M, Y)$ of a CMY distribution nor its density function can be derived in a closed form, we must rely on numerical Laplace inversion techniques.

7.5   LÉVY BASE CORRELATION

7.5.1   The Concept of Base Correlation

The concept of Lévy base correlation (BC) was introduced and illustrated with the Gamma model in Garcia *et al.* (2008). The procedure of bootstrapping BCs in the Lévy case is exactly the same as in the Gaussian, since the only difference relies on the underlying process. Information on the BC of lower tranches is used to derive the BC of less risky tranches, as follows:

- We start with the equity tranche ([0%–3%]) and solve for ρ, such that the model price matches the market quote. The ρ obtained, say $\rho_{[0\%-3\%]}$, is the so-called equity Lévy BC.
- Next, we focus on the [3%–6%] tranche. In the fair spread formula of this tranche, the expected percentage loss of the [3%–6%] tranche is obtained in terms of the percentage expected loss of the [0%–6%] and the [0%–3%] tranches. To calculate the percentage expected loss of the [0%–3%] tranche, we use the value $\rho_{[0\%-3\%]}$. Next, we solve for the Lévy BC $\rho_{[0\%-6\%]}$ in order to calculate the percentage expected loss of the [0%–6%] tranche, so that the [3%–6%] tranche spread matches exactly the market spread.
- We proceed in the same manner through the higher tranches.

Note that compared to the Gaussian case, under the Lévy setting for some models we might have additional distribution parameters. There are two alternative ways to choose these distribution parameters. One could take the parameters from a global calibration, or one could just set them equal to some value. The pros and cons of these two approaches were discussed in Garcia *et al.* (2008).

Here we study several cases: the Gamma(1), IG(1.5), and CMY(0.5; 0.5) Lévy BC models. Table 7.1 summarizes the properties of the chosen models.

Typical base correlation curves are shown in Figure 7.3 for the Gaussian and Gamma processes. Lévy BC curves are typically much flatter than Gaussian curves (Figure 7.4).

The evolution of the BC over time for [0%–3%] and [12%–22%] tranches is presented in Figure 7.5 for the Gaussian model and the three Lévy models of Table 7.1. One can see that the dynamics of the BC is very similar for all the models. We have also plotted the BC curve for the Gamma(a) model, where the

Table 7.1   Properties of the Gamma(1), IG(1.5), and CMY(0.5; 0.5) Lévy BC models

	Gamma(1)	IG(1.5)	CMY(0.5; 0.5)
Variance	1	1	1
Skewness	2	2.3	2.6
Kurtosis	9	12	14

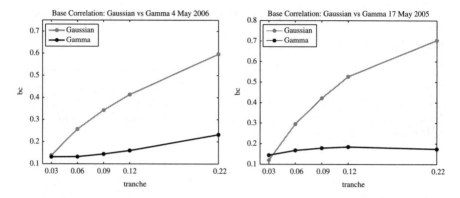

Figure 7.3   Base Correlation Curve

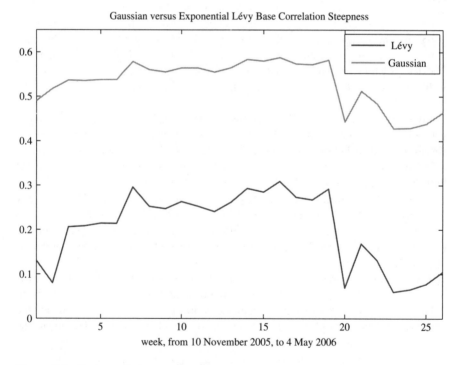

Figure 7.4   Base correlation steepness

gamma parameter a is taken differently from day to day and comes from a global calibration. We note that the steepness of the BC curve does not increase very much: the steepness of the Gamma(1) BC curve is, on average, 1.2 times higher than that of the Gamma(a) (compared to the steepness of the Gaussian BC curve which, on average, is 4 times higher than that of the Gamma(a)).

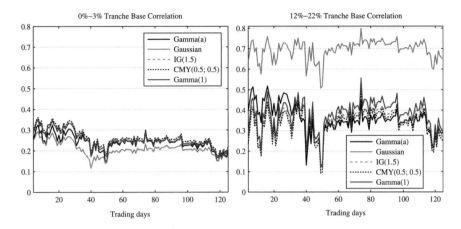

Figure 7.5 Base correlation of the [0%–3%] and [12%–22%] tranches–iTraxx data 21-03-2005–20-09-2005

7.5.2 Pricing Non-Standard Tranches

The BC construction is quite useful to price non-standard tranches. Suppose we want to price a [5%–10%] tranche of the iTraxx portfolio. With the base correlation methodology, this requires a BC value for the [0%–10%] tranche and for the [0%–5%] tranche. However, the market information only gives us the base correlations for the [0%–3%], [0%–6%], [0%–9%], [0%–12%] and [0%–22%] tranches (see, for example, the values in Table 7.2).

Using linear interpolation between these values, the Gaussian BC for a [0%–5%] tranche is

$$\rho_{[0\%-5\%]}^{(\text{Gauss})} = \frac{1}{3} \times \rho_{[0\%-3\%]}^{(\text{Gauss})} + \frac{2}{3} \times \rho_{[0\%-6\%]}^{(\text{Gauss})}$$

$$= \frac{1}{3} \times 0.1388 + \frac{2}{3} \times 0.2570 = 0.2176.$$

For the Lévy case we have

$$\rho_{[0\%-5\%]}^{(\text{Lévy})} = \frac{1}{3} \times \rho_{[0\%-3\%]}^{(\text{Lévy})} + \frac{2}{3} \times \rho_{[0\%-6\%]}^{(\text{Lévy})}$$

$$= \frac{1}{3} \times 0.1315 + \frac{2}{3} \times 0.1326 = 0.1322.$$

Table 7.2 Base correlation values

Model	[0%–3%]	[0%–6%]	[0%–9%]	[0%–12%]	[0%–22%]
Gaussian	0.1388	0.2570	0.3428	0.4134	0.5956
Lévy	0.1315	0.1326	0.1447	0.1602	0.2318

The Gaussian BC for the [0%–10%] tranche is

$$\rho_{[0\%-10\%]}^{(\text{Gauss})} = \frac{2}{3} \times \rho_{[0\%-9\%]}^{(\text{Gauss})} + \frac{1}{3} \times \rho_{[0\%-12\%]}^{(\text{Gauss})}$$

$$= \frac{2}{3} \times 0.3428 + \frac{1}{3} \times 0.4134 = 0.3663.$$

For the Lévy case we have

$$\rho_{[0\%-10\%]}^{(\text{Lévy})} = \frac{2}{3} \times \rho_{[0\%-9\%]}^{(\text{Lévy})} + \frac{1}{3} \times \rho_{[0\%-12\%]}^{(\text{Lévy})}$$

$$= \frac{2}{3} \times 0.1447 + \frac{1}{3} \times 0.1602 = 0.1498.$$

Using these values one can price the [0%–10%] tranche. The Gaussian case leads to a price of 12.47 bp whereas the Lévy model price is much higher at 14.74 bp. Note that the procedure is also sensitive to the interpolation scheme. A spline interpolation, gives

$$\rho_{[0\%-5\%]}^{(\text{Gauss})} = 0.2222 \text{ vs } 0.2176$$

$$\rho_{[0\%-5\%]}^{(\text{Lévy})} = 0.1306 \text{ vs } 0.1322$$

$$\rho_{[0\%-10\%]}^{(\text{Gauss})} = 0.3675 \text{ vs } 0.3663$$

$$\rho_{[0\%-10\%]}^{(\text{Lévy})} = 0.1496 \text{ vs } 0.1498.$$

This combination leads to a price of 14.00 bps (vs 12.47 bps) and 14.13 bps (vs 14.74 bps) under Gaussian and Lévy, respectively.

Let us also explore tranchlets (i.e. very thin tranches) of width 0.5% and price them under the four models mentioned above: the Gaussian, the Gamma(1), the IG(1.5) and CMY(0.5; 0.5). We calculate tranchlet prices using two different interpolation methods: (a) the simplest linear interpolation, and (b) more advanced spline interpolation. Results are plotted in Figure 7.6 where we observe that using linear interpolation in the Gaussian setting, one can, for example, buy protection for the [5.5%–6%] tranche around 50 bps and sell protection for the [6%–6.5%] tranche with higher seniority for around 80 bps. This is an arbitrage situation, since the more senior the tranche, the less risky and hence the lower the fair spread must be. These kinds of arbitrage situations occur much less frequently in the Lévy settings.

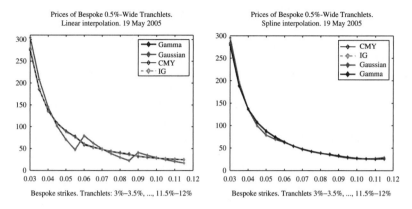

Figure 7.6 Lévy vs Gaussian prices of bespoke half of a percent wide tranchlets – iTraxx data 19-05-2005

7.5.3 Correlation Mapping for Bespoke CDOs

On top of the above described interpolation on the base correlation curve, a current market approach for the pricing of tranches of so-called bespoke CDOs is based on the concept of correlation mapping. One extracts out of the base correlation curve of a liquid standardized CDO (iTraxx, CDX, ...) the base correlation to price tranches for the bespoke CDO.

A simple but extremely naive way, is to take the base correlation $\rho_{\text{Bespoke}}(A)$ for a certain attachment point, A, on the bespoke CDO equal to the base correlation $\rho(A)$ for the same attachment point in the standardized CDO:

$$\rho_{\text{Bespoke}}(A) = \rho(A).$$

There are many more sophisticated mappings. Here we only mention the most common practice. The mapping takes into account the bespoke portfolio expected loss $\mathbb{E}[L_{\text{Bespoke}}^{[0\%-100\%]}]$ and compares this with the available standardized CDO expected loss $\mathbb{E}[L^{[0\%-100\%]}]$. The correlation for the attachment point A for the bespoke CDO is given by:

$$\rho_{\text{Bespoke}}(A) = \rho\left(A \times \frac{\mathbb{E}[L_{\text{Bespoke}}^{[0\%-100\%]}]}{\mathbb{E}[L^{[0\%-100\%]}]}\right).$$

If the bespoke and the standardized portfolios have the same expected losses, the bespoke base correlation curve will be the same as the base correlation of the standardized CDO. Care has to be taken, because this kind of mapping does not take into account the dispersion of spreads in the portfolio.

7.6   DELTA-HEDGING CDO TRANCHES

A tranche investor often hedges its position (dynamically) using a technique called 'delta-hedging'. Delta-hedging involves offsetting the impact of changing spread levels on the tranche value by buying protection in a CDS index or single-name CDSs in an appropriate fraction of the tranche's notional amount. This specific fraction is called 'delta'. As spreads fluctuate, deltas also change, and the hedge must be frequently adjusted.

There are three common approaches to hedge a CDO tranche. First, to hedge a tranche with the index; second, to hedge a tranche using a single-name CDS and finally to hedge a tranche with another tranche (for example, to hedge a long position in the equity tranche and buy a short position in the junior mezzanine). Calculation of deltas, and hence implementation of a hedging strategy, is entirely model-dependent. In this section we study and compare hedge parameters of the four different base correlation models: Gaussian, Gamma, IG and CMY.

In order to determine these deltas, we need the *risky annuity* (RA) and *mark-to-market* (MTM) concepts. As mentioned before, the risky annuity of a tranche is the present value of 1 bp of spread paid over the life of the contract. The mark-to-market for a long-risk tranche trade is expressed as

$$\text{MTM}_{\text{current}} = (s_{\text{initial}} - s_{\text{current}}) \cdot \text{RA}_{\text{current}}.$$

7.6.1   Hedging with the CDS Index

In order to delta-hedge a tranche with the CDS index, we need to calculate a 'delta' for the tranche. Theoretically, a delta for the tranche determines the size of the hedge required and is calculated as a ratio of the tranche's mark-to-market change to that of the CDS index position, given a 1-bp parallel shift in the average of all CDS spreads in the reference pool,

$$\Delta_{\text{index}} = \frac{\text{MTM}^{\text{Tranche}}_{\text{indexShift}} - \text{MTM}^{\text{Tranche}}_{\text{current}}}{\text{MTM}^{\text{index}}_{\text{indexShift}} - \text{MTM}^{\text{index}}_{\text{current}}}.$$

Figure 7.7 shows variation of the equity and junior mezzanine deltas over time. One can see that deltas obtained under the introduced Lévy base correlation models are completely consistent with Gaussian deltas, i.e. delta curves are roughly moving in parallel.

7.6.2   Delta-Hedging with a Single-Name CDS

In order to delta-hedge a tranche with a single-name CDS, we need to calculate a delta for the tranche as the ratio of the tranche's mark-to-market change to that of

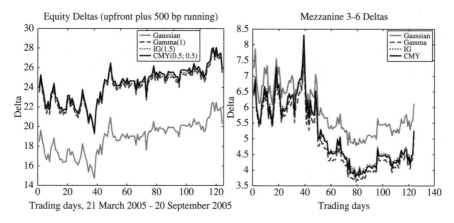

Figure 7.7   Equity and junior mezzanine deltas for different models – iTraxx data

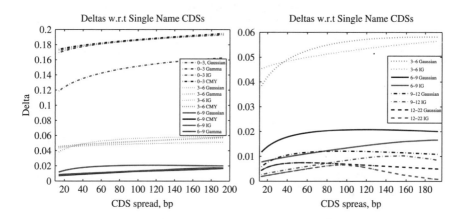

Figure 7.8   Deltas with respect to single-name CDSs – iTraxx data 19-05-2005

the single-name CDS, given a 1-bp parallel shift in the underlying spread curve of the CDS,

$$\Delta_{\text{CDS}} = \frac{\text{MTM}_{\text{CDSshift}}^{\text{Tranche}} - \text{MTM}_{\text{current}}^{\text{Tranche}}}{\text{MTM}_{\text{CDSshift}}^{\text{CDS}} - \text{MTM}_{\text{current}}^{\text{CDS}}}$$

Figure 7.8 illustrates equity and mezzanine deltas with respect to single-name CDS entering the iTraxx index for all the models under investigation. One can see that, similar to deltas with respect to an index, deltas with respect to single-name CDSs under all the Lévy models are almost equal in values.

7.6.3 Mezz-Equity Hedging

Mezz-equity hedging is a hedging strategy which involves selling protection on the equity tranche and buying protection on the first mezzanine tranche, or the other way around. The theoretical hedge ratio between two tranches can be expressed as

$$\text{HedgeRatio}_{\text{mezz}-\text{equity}} = \frac{\Delta_{\text{index}}^{\text{equity}}}{\Delta_{\text{index}}^{\text{mezzanine}}},$$

i.e. the hedge ratio is the ratio of the equity tranche MTM change to that of the mezzanine, given a 1-bp parallel shift in the underlying spread curve of the index.

Figure 7.9 shows the evolution of the hedge ratios over time. Lévy hedge ratios, and thus typical trading strategies based on these ratios, can be very different from the Gaussian ones.

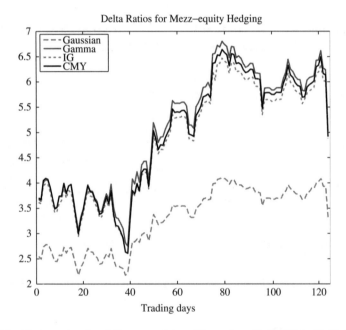

Figure 7.9   Hedge ratios for different models – iTraxx data 21-03-2005–20-09-2005

8
Multivariate Index Modelling

In this chapter, we will set up some models for index spread dynamics. We will first start with the traditional Black's model and then generalize to jump-driven models. Finally, we arrive at jump-driven multivariate index models. As a working example, we will model four indices simultaneously (all with a 5-year term), namely iTraxx Europe Main, iTraxx HiVol, CDX.NA.IG Main and CDX.NA.HiVol.

The spreads of the indices (giving protection to all components) are highly correlated with each other, as can be seen in Figure 8.1. This correlation is often important in typically CPPI and CPDO structures (see Chapter 9) based on a combination of positions in several indices.

The models will be calibrated on the available swaption market and matched with a historical correlation matrix. To calculate swaption prices under the advanced jump models, we will make use of characteristic functions and Fast Fourier Transform (FFT) techniques.

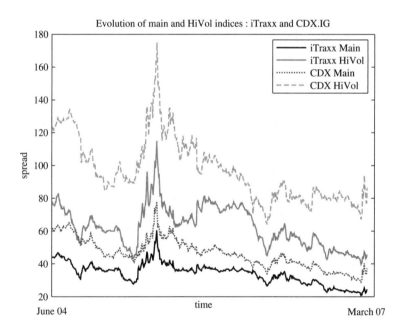

Figure 8.1 Correlated credit indices

8.1 BLACK'S MODEL

The market standard for modelling credit spreads and pricing swaptions is a modi-
fication of Black's model for interest rates (see Pederson 2004).

It models spread dynamics in a Black–Scholes fashion:

$$S_t(T^*) = S_0(T^*) \exp(-\sigma^2 t/2 + \sigma W_t), \quad t \geq 0, \tag{8.1}$$

where T^* refers to the credit index swap maturity and $\sigma > 0$ is the spread volatility.

Let us introduce some notation. Denote by T the (payer or receiver) swaption
maturity (typically 3, 6, or 9 months), which is usually much smaller than T^*, the
credit index maturity (typically 5, 7 or 10 years). Let us denote with $A(0, t)$ the
risky annuity for maturity t (i.e. the present value of 1 bp of the fee leg), and with
$A(T, T^*)$ the forward annuity, i.e. $A(T, T^*) = A(0, T^*) - A(0, T)$.

Under the above Black's spread dynamics, one can price swaptions (Payer,
Receivers, ...). Black's formula for a swaption with maturity T and strike K
simplifies to

$$\text{Payer}(T, K) = A(T, T^*) \times (F_0^{(\text{adj})} \Phi(d_1) - K \Phi(d_2))$$

$$\text{Receiver}(T, K) = A(T, T^*) \times (K \Phi(-d_2) - F_0^{(\text{adj})} \Phi(-d_1)).$$

where Φ is the usual standard Normal cumulative distribution function, $F_0^{(\text{adj})}$ is
the adjusted for no-knockout forward spread (for details see below) and

$$d_1 = \frac{\log\left(F_0^{(\text{adj})}/K\right) + \sigma^2 T/2}{\sigma\sqrt{T}} \quad \text{and } d_2 = d_1 - \sigma\sqrt{T}.$$

The forward spread between T and T^* is calculated in the usual fashion:

$$F_0(T, T^*) = \frac{S_0(T^*)A(0, T^*) - S_0(T)A(0, T)}{A(0, T^*) - A(0, T)}.$$

However, we adjust the forward to account for the 'No Knockout' feature of the
swaption: if a name in the index defaults before expiry of the swaption, we will
enter into an index with a defaulted name at expiry of the swaption. We account for
this additional protection by increasing the forward spread by the cost of protection
over that extra period $[0, T]$:

$$F_0^{(\text{adj})}(T, T^*) = F_0(T, T^*) + \frac{S_0(T)A(0, T)}{A(0, T^*) - A(0, T)}$$

$$= \frac{S_0(T^*)A(0, T^*)}{A(0, T^*) - A(0, T)}$$

$$= \frac{\text{PV}^{\text{Loss}}(T^*)}{A(T, T^*)}$$

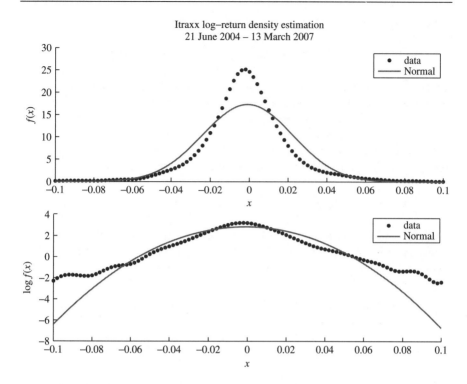

Figure 8.2   Empirical density of iTraxx Main (on the run) log returns versus a normal density

Note that in Black's formula there is a striking connection with vanilla option prices in equity. However, the model also has all the deficiencies of the Black–Scholes model (e.g. Black's model assumes very light tails for the daily changes in the spread). As we have witnessed in, for example, the credit crunch, credit market events are very shock driven. Jumps and heavy tails are therefore important features to take into account in the modelling. In Figure 8.2, we plot the empirical density of log-returns of the iTraxx Main (on the run) index together with a plot of a Normal density (with same mean and variance as the empirical one) and also the log density, which gives a better view near the tails. We observe that the empirical density has a rather linear decay of the log density in contrast to the Normal density where there is a quadratic decay of the log of the density.

8.2   VG CREDIT SPREAD MODEL

Next, we describe a jump-driven Lévy model for index spread dynamics. The model is based on results published in Garcia *et al.* (2008). As in the equity setting, we replace the Black–Scholes dynamics with the better performing jump dynamics of a Lévy process. We work out the details for the VG process (see Section 2.3.6).

More precisely, we model the spread dynamics as

$$S_t(T^*) = S_0(T^*) \exp(\omega t + \theta G_t + \sigma W_{G_t}) = S_0(T^*) \exp(\omega t + X_t),$$

where $\omega = v^{-1} \log(1 - \frac{1}{2}\sigma^2 v - \theta v)$ assures that $\mathbb{E}[S_t(T^*)] = S_0(T^*)$. The pricing of vanillas (using the Carr–Madan formula in combination with FFT methods) has already worked out in full detail in equity settings (see Carr and Madan (1999)). Here the procedure is adapted to credit spread dynamics.

The main ingredient in the pricing formula is the characteristic function of the logarithm of the adjusted forwards spread at the swaption maturity T.

$$\phi(u; T) = E\left[\exp\left(iu\left(\log F_0^{(adj)} + \omega T + X_T\right)\right)\right],$$

which is known analytically in the VG case and for many other Lévy dynamics.

Swaptions are priced using the Carr–Madan formula (see Carr and Madan 1999) modified for a credit spread setting:

$$\text{Payer}(T, K) = A(T, T^*) \times \frac{\exp(-\alpha \log(K))}{\pi}$$

$$\times \int_0^{+\infty} \exp(-iv \log(K)) \frac{\phi(v - (\alpha + 1)i; T)}{\alpha^2 + \alpha - v^2 + i(2\alpha + 1)v} dv,$$

where α is a positive constant such that the αth moment of the spread price exists. We will comment later on the choice of α.

8.3   PRICING SWAPTIONS USING FFT

In this section we describe how one can price very fast and efficiently swaptions using the theory of characteristic functions and FFT. The methodology is almost identical to the valuation problem of vanillas in equity. FFT is an efficient algorithm for computing the following transformation of a vector $(\alpha_n, n = 1, \ldots, N)$ into a vector $(\beta_n, n = 1, \ldots, N)$:

$$\beta_n = \sum_{j=1}^N \exp\left(-\frac{i2\pi(j-1)(n-1)}{N}\right) \alpha_j.$$

Typically, N is a power of 2. The number of operations of the FFT algorithm is of the order $\mathcal{O}(N \log N)$ and this in contrast to the straightforward evaluation of the above sums which give rise to $\mathcal{O}(N^2)$ numbers of operations.

Denote with $k = \log(K)$ and let

$$\varrho(v) = \frac{\phi(v - (\alpha + 1)i; T)}{\alpha^2 + \alpha - v^2 + i(2\alpha + 1)v}.$$

An approximation for the integral in the Carr–Madan formula

$$I(k, T) = \int_0^\infty \exp(-ivk)\varrho(v)\,dv$$

on the N points grid $(0, \eta, 2\eta, 3\eta, \ldots, (N-1)\eta)$ is

$$I(k, T) \approx \sum_{j=1}^{N} \exp(-iv_j k)\varrho(v_j)\eta, \quad v_j = \eta(j-1).$$

We will calculate the value of $I(k_n, T)$ for N log-strikes levels k_n ranging from, say, $-b$ to b (note: if $S_0 = 1$, at-the-money corresponds to $b = 0$):

$$k_n = -b + \lambda(n-1), \quad n = 1, \ldots, N, \quad \text{where } \lambda = 2b/N.$$

This gives

$$I(k_n, T) \approx \sum_{j=1}^{N} \exp(-iv_j(-b + \lambda(n-1)))\varrho(v_j)\eta,$$

$$= \sum_{j=1}^{N} \exp(-i\eta\lambda(j-1)(n-1)) \exp(iv_j b)\varrho(v_j)\eta.$$

If we choose λ and η such that $\lambda\eta = 2\pi/N$, then

$$I(k_n, T) \approx \sum_{j=1}^{N} \exp\left(-\frac{i2\pi(j-1)(n-1)}{N}\right) \exp(iv_j b)\varrho(v_j)\eta.$$

The above summation is an exact application of the FFT on the vector

$$(\exp(iv_j b)\varrho(v_j)\eta, \quad j = 1, \ldots, N).$$

Note that by fixing $\lambda\eta = 2\pi/N$, taking a smaller grid size η makes the grid size λ (for the log-strike grid) larger. Carr and Madan (1999) report that the following choice gave very satisfactory results:

$$\eta = 0.25, \quad N = 4096, \quad \alpha = 1.5,$$

which implies

$$\lambda = 0.0061, \quad b = 12.57.$$

A more refined weighting (Simpson's rule) for the integral in the Carr–Madan formula on the N points grid $(0, \eta, 2\eta, 3\eta, \ldots, (N-1)\eta)$ leads to the following approximation

$$I(k_n, T) \approx \sum_{j=1}^{N} \exp(-iv_j k_n) \varrho(v_j) \eta \left(\frac{3 + (-1)^j - \delta_{j-1}}{3} \right), \quad v_j = \eta(j-1)$$

and gives a more accurate integration.

All the above leads to an approximation for the price of payer swaptions for a range of log-strikes $k_n, n = 1, \ldots, N$ carefully chosen in order to make the FFT work:

$$\text{Payer}(T, \exp(k_n)) \approx A(T, T^*) \exp(-\alpha k_n)$$

$$\times \frac{1}{\pi} \sum_{j=1}^{N} \exp(-iv_j k_n) \varrho(v_j) \eta \left(\frac{3 + (-1)^j - \delta_{j-1}}{3} \right).$$

For a given strike K, we can interpolate on the grid $\{k_n, n = 1, \ldots, N\}$ to obtain the value of the payer for the desired log-strike $k = \log(K)$.

8.4 MULTIVARIATE VG MODEL

Next, we will extend the above VG model to a multivariate setting. To build such a Multivariate Variance Gamma (MVG) model, we need several ingredients:

- a common Gamma process $G = \{G_t, t \geq 0\}$ with parameters $a = b = 1/v$;
- a N-dimensional Brownian motion $\vec{W} = \{(W_t^{(1)}, \ldots, W_t^{(N)}), t \geq 0\}$.

We assume that $\vec{W}$ is independent of G and that the Brownian motions have a correlation matrix:

$$\rho_{ij}^W = \mathbb{E}[W_1^{(i)} W_1^{(j)}] = \text{Corr}[W_1^{(i)} W_1^{(j)}].$$

The above construction is based on related work by Luciano and Schoutens (2006) and Leoni and Schoutens (2008).

A multivariate VG process $\vec{X} = \{(X_t^{(1)}, \ldots, X_t^{(N)}), t \geq 0\}$ is defined as:

$$X_t^{(i)} = \theta_i G_t + \sigma_i W_{G_t}^{(i)}, \quad t \geq 0.$$

There is dependency between the $X_t^{(i)}$'s due to two causes. Firstly, the processes are all constructed by time-changing with a common Gamma time. Secondly, dependency is also built in via the Brownian motions.

The correlation between two components is given by:

$$\rho_{ij} = \frac{\mathbb{E}[X_1^{(i)} X_1^{(j)}] - \mathbb{E}[X_1^{(i)}]\mathbb{E}[X_1^{(j)}]}{\sqrt{\mathrm{Var}[X_1^{(i)}]}\sqrt{\mathrm{Var}[X_1^{(j)}]}}$$

$$= \frac{\theta_i \theta_j v + \sigma_i \sigma_j \rho_{ij}^W}{\sqrt{\sigma_i^2 + \theta_i^2 v}\sqrt{\sigma_j^2 + \theta_j^2 v}}.$$

The fact that this correlation is closed form available, makes it possible to match the model correlation with a given a prescribed correlation.

We use the MVG processes to describe the evolution of N correlated spreads (all with the same index maturity T^* for simplicity):

$$S_t^{(i)}(T^*) = S_0^{(i)}(T^*) \exp(\omega_i t + \theta_i G_t + \sigma_i W_{G_t}^{(i)}), \quad i = 1, \ldots, N,$$

where

$$\omega_i = v^{-1} \log\left(1 - \frac{1}{2}\sigma_i^2 v - \theta_i v\right).$$

The parameters v, θ_i and σ_i are coming from a (joint) calibration on swaptions on the individual spreads. Then ρ_{ij}^W is set to match a prespecified (e.g. historical) correlation ρ_{ij} between the spreads:

$$\rho_{ij}^W = \frac{\rho_{ij}\sqrt{\sigma_i^2 + \theta_i^2 v}\sqrt{\sigma_j^2 + \theta_j^2 v} - \theta_i \theta_j v}{\sigma_i \sigma_j}.$$

Let us illustrate this and work out the details on a joint model of four indices: iTraxx Europe Main, iTraxx HiVol, CDX.NA.IG Main and CDX.NA.HiVol. We assume the following correlated VG dynamics for the spreads:

$$S_t^{(\text{iTraxx Main})}(T^*) = S_0^{(\text{iTraxx Main})}(T^*) \exp(\omega_1 t + \theta_1 G_t + \sigma_1 W_{G_t}^{(1)})$$

$$S_t^{(\text{iTraxx HiVol})}(T^*) = S_0^{(\text{iTraxx HiVol})}(T^*) \exp(\omega_2 t + \theta_2 G_t + \sigma_2 W_{G_t}^{(2)})$$

$$S_t^{(\text{CDX Main})}(T^*) = S_0^{(\text{CDX Main})}(T^*) \exp(\omega_3 t + \theta_3 G_t + \sigma_3 W_{G_t}^{(3)})$$

$$S_t^{(\text{CDX HiVol})}(T^*) = S_0^{(\text{CDX HiVol})}(T^*) \exp(\omega_4 t + \theta_4 G_t + \sigma_4 W_{G_t}^{(4)}),$$

where G_t is a common Gamma process, such that $G_t \sim \mathrm{Gamma}(t/v, 1/v)$, and the $W_t^{(i)}$'s are correlated standard Brownian motions with a given correlation matrix ρ^W.

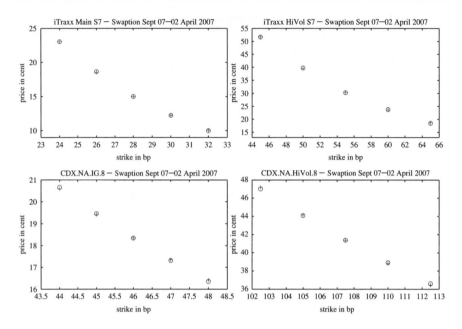

Figure 8.3   Joint calibration on swaptions of credit indices

Table 8.1   Correlation of log-returns: iTraxx (Main and HiVol) and CDX (Main and HiVol)

Correlation	iTtraxx Main	iTraxx HiVol	CDX Main	CDX HiVol
iTraxx Main	1.0000	0.9258	0.4719	0.3339
iTraxx HiVol	0.9258	1.0000	0.4398	0.3281
CDX Main	0.4719	0.4398	1.0000	0.8580
CDX HiVol	0.3339	0.3281	0.8580	1.0000

First calibrate (with a common ν parameter) the individual spread dynamics on a series of swaptions. The resulting fit is given in Figure 8.3 (o-signs are market prices, +-signs are the model prices).

Then match with the required correlation. In our working example, we take the historical correlation of the log-returns over the period from 21 June 2004 to 13 March 2007; the values are given in Table 8.1.

To do that, set the Brownian correlation matrix equal to:

$$\rho^W = \begin{bmatrix} 1.0000 & 0.9265 & 0.4935 & 0.3352 \\ 0.9265 & 1.0000 & 0.4470 & 0.3247 \\ 0.4935 & 0.4470 & 1.0000 & 0.8688 \\ 0.3352 & 0.3247 & 0.8688 & 1.0000 \end{bmatrix}$$

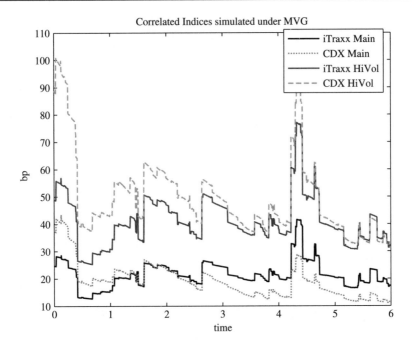

Figure 8.4 Multivariate VG paths for the modelling of correlated credit indices

Note that the ρ^W matrix calculated in the above fashion is not necessary positive-definite. In such a situation, one can then, as a kind of *ad-hoc* method, look for the closed positive-definite matrix and work with that one.

Simulation of Gamma processes and correlated Brownian motions is easy and opens the way to exotic basket option pricing on credit indices. In Figure 8.4, one sees a simulation of the four indices modelled above.

Part IV
Exotic Structured Credit Risk Products

9
Credit CPPIs and CPDOs

9.1 INTRODUCTION

In recent years we have seen a huge growth of structured credit derivatives. One such innovation is a credit *Constant Proportion Portfolio Insurance* (CPPI). A credit CPPI is a capital guaranteed (principal protected) investment strategy and in its simplest format works just like a capital protected credit-linked note. The invested capital is put in a risk-free bond and a position is taken on credit derivatives (usually one is long risk, meaning that protection is sold) in the form of a basket and more recently using standardized corporate CDO indices (iTraxx/CDX). Intrinsic to the price of a CPPI is the so-called *gap risk*, i.e. the risk of spread jumps of the underlying credit indices on which the short positions are taken and which could cause losses to the deal structurer. A different structured derivative is represented by the *Constant Proportion Debt Obligation* (CPDO). These instruments do not offer principal protection, but aim for a high rating (typically AAA) and fix a present return which is sought to be reached. If the target is reached, risky positions are closed.

In this chapter we use the multivariate VG-based dynamic spread models introduced in the previous chapter to analyze CPPI and CPDO structures. The parameters of the model come from a two-step calibration procedure. First, by a joint calibration on swaptions payers and, second, by a correlation matching procedure. In the joint calibration step we made use of equity-like pricing formulas for payers and receivers based on characteristic functions and Fast Fourier Transform methods as described in Chapter 8. To obtain the required correlation, we also employ the approach described in Chapter 8: we use a closed-form matching procedure such that the model's correlation is matched to a prescribed (e.g. historical) correlation. The model put in place is capable of generating very fast correlated spread dynamics under jump dynamics. We illustrate this by pricing the current popular credit CPPI structures and analyse and rate a CPDO deal. The built in jump dynamics makes it possible to have a better assessment of gap risk.

Some other reference on CPPIs and CPDOs in the literature are Bertrand and Prigent (2002, 2003, 2005) and Cont and Tankov (2007).

9.2 CPPIs

The Constant Proportion Portfolio Insurance (CPPI) was first introduced by Fisher Black and Robert Jones (1987). Recently, credit-linked CPPIs have become popular to create capital protected credit-linked notes. CPPI products are leveraged investments whose returns depend on the performance of an underlying trading strategy. Quite often positions are taken into the available credit indices (iTraxx, CDX, ...). Credit CPPIs combine dynamic leverage with principal protection. Specifically, the strategy invests on a safe account in order to guarantee that, at maturity, the capital can be paid back, and then takes risky positions (short and/or long) on credit products. Leverage is increased when the strategy performs well and is reduced when it performs poorly. We illustrate the details of such a product by an example, where positions will be taken in four highly correlated indices and a predefined trading strategy is in place.

In our example, we take positions in the following index products:

- iTraxx Europe Main on the run (5 years)
- iTraxx Europe HiVol on the run (5 years)
- DJ CDX.NA.IG Main on the run (5 years)
- DJ CDX.NA.IG HiVol on the run (5 years)

The swap rates for the above products are highly correlated. The strategy is to sell protection on the 5-year on-the-run Main indices for half of the risky exposure (defined and calculated below) each, and to buy protection on the 5-year on-the-run HiVol subsets for $\zeta \frac{1}{2} \frac{30}{125}$ of the risky exposure. The parameter ζ can be positive as well as negative; the fraction $\frac{1}{2}$ comes from the fact that we take position in two HiVol indices; the fraction $\frac{30}{125}$ stems from the fact that 30 out of 125 names of the Main indices are part of the HiVol indices. The corresponding correlation matrix of the daily log-returns based on observations from 21 June 2004 until 13 March 2007 is given in Table 8.1.

The following factors play a key role in the CPPI investment strategy:

- The initial investment N and the maturity T.
- The current *value* of the CPPI. The value at time $t \in [0, T]$ will be denoted as V_t. We have $V_0 = N$.
- The *floor* is the reference level to which the value of the CPPI is compared. This level will guarantee the possibility of repaying the fixed amount N at maturity T. Hence, it could be seen as the present value of N at maturity. Typically this is a risk-free bank account and its price at time t will be denoted as $B_t = \exp(-r(T - t))N$.
- The *cushion*, C_t, is defined as the difference between the price and the floor: $C_t = V_t - B_t$.
- The multiplier m is a fixed value which represents the amount of leverage an investor is willing to take.
- The risky exposure is given by: $E_t = m \times C_t$. Note that the dynamic leverage is related to the fact that C_t fluctuates over time (while m stays constant). Moreover, note that the leverage increases the more the portfolio performs well, i.e. the higher is the difference between V_t and B_t.

The investor will take a non-negative risky exposure at each time t as long as the value of the CPPI exceeds the floor. For any time t the future investment decision will be made according to the following rule:

- if $V_t \leq B_t$, we will invest the complete portfolio into a risk-free bank account,
- if $V_t > B_t$, we will take a risky exposure calculated below on the basis of the amount E_t.

Say, we start with a portfolio of $N = 100$m EUR and have an investment horizon of $T = 6$ years and let $\zeta = 1/10$. We want to have the principal of the initial investment protected. Therefore, we calculate the *bond floor* as the value of a risk-free bond that matures at the end of the investment horizon. Suppose we take $r = 4\%$ and use compound interest rates, then the bond floor is initially at $B_0 = 78.6628$m EUR. Suppose we set the leverage at $m = 25$. We called the *cushion* the difference between the portfolio value and the bond floor. Initially, the cushion is thus at $C_0 = 21.3372$m EUR. Multiplying the cushion with the constant leverage factor of 25, gives the risky exposure that we are going to take, namely $E_0 = 533.43$m EUR. We then are taking the following positions:

- sell protection on iTraxx Europe Main for half of the risky exposure (266.715m EUR);
- buy protection on iTraxx Europe HiVol for $\frac{1}{10}\frac{1}{2}\frac{30}{125}$ of the risky exposure (6.40116m EUR);
- sell protection on DJ CDX.NA.IG Main for half of the risky exposure (266.715m EUR);
- buy protection on DJ CDX.NA.IG HiVol for $\frac{1}{10}\frac{1}{2}\frac{30}{125}$ of the risky exposure (6.40116m EUR).

We thus sell protection on all the companies in the Main CDX and iTraxx index, and buy back a fraction (10%) of protection for the ones in the HiVol segment. So actually our true exposure is, in this example, a bit smaller than E_t. To be precise we have sold protection on a total notional amount of 520.62768m EUR. Of course other weighting could be possible.

The initial 100m EUR is put on a risk-free bank account at a compound rate of 4%.

Suppose the current quotes for the four components of our portfolio are those given in Table 9.1. We normally rebalance each day. However, for the sake of explanation, assume that we do not change our position for a quarter (and no defaults occurred). After the first quarter our bank account would have grown to 101.0050m EUR. Further, we then would have received/paid fee income/payments

- on iTraxx Europe Main for the amount: $0.0024625 \times 266.7150/4 = 0.1642$m EUR
- on iTraxx Europe HiVol for the amount: $-0.004875 \times 6.40116/4 = -0.007800$m EUR

Table 9.1 Quotes used for the four components of our portfolio in bp

	$t = 0$
iTraxx Main	24.625
iTraxx HiVol	48.75
CDX Main	37.5
CDX HiVol	88.5

- on DJ CDX.NA.IG Main for the amount: $0.00375 \times 266.7150/4 = 0.2500$m EUR
- on DJ CDX.NA.IG HiVol for the amount: $-0.00885 \times 6.401160/4 = -0.01416$m EUR

Leading to a total spread income after 3 months of: 0.39224m EUR.

Suppose that we then rebalance (note that actually one should do this on a daily basis). Suppose that the spreads for our components have moved as in Table 9.2. This movements of the spreads has the following mark-to-market effect. We assume that we always have a risky annuity of 4.5:

- on iTraxx Europe Main: $4.5 \times (0.0024625 - 0.0021625) \times 266.7150 = 0.3601$m EUR;
- on iTraxx Europe HiVol: $-4.5 \times (0.004875 - 0.003875) \times 6.40116 = -0.02881$m EUR;
- on DJ CDX.NA.IG Main: $4.5 \times (0.00375 - 0.00325) \times 266.7150 = 0.6001$m EUR;
- on DJ CDX.NA.IG HiVol: $-4.5 \times (0.00885 - 0.00755) \times 6.40116 = -0.03745$m EUR.

Hence, the total mark-to-market change is equal to 0.89394m EUR.

This means that after one quarter the CPPI value of the portfolio has grown to $101.0050 + 0.39224 + 0.89394 = 102.29118$m EUR. The bond floor is then at

Table 9.2 Quotes used for the four components of our portfolio in bp

	$t = 0$	$t = 3$ months
iTraxx Main	24.625	21.625
iTraxx HiVol	48.75	38.75
CDX Main	37.5	32.5
CDX HiVol	88.5	75.5

79.4534m EUR and hence the cushion at $102.29118 - 79.4534 = 22.83778$m EUR. The allowed risky exposure is recalculated to be $22.83778 \times 25 = 570.9445$m EUR and we rebalance such that the total position is now given by

- sold protection on iTraxx Europe Main for half of the risky exposure, i.e. for 285.47225m EUR;
- bought protection on iTraxx Europe HiVol for $\frac{1}{10}\frac{1}{2}\frac{30}{125}$ the risky exposure, i.e. for 6.851334m EUR;
- sold protection on DJ CDX.NA.IG Main for half of the risky exposure, i.e. for 285.47225m EUR;
- bought protection on DJ CDX.NA.IG HiVol for $\frac{1}{10}\frac{1}{2}\frac{30}{125}$ of the risky exposure, i.e. for 6.851334m EUR.

We continue doing this until maturity or until we have a negative cushion at a rebalancing date. In that case all positions are closed. Then, however, we cannot always pay back the principal amount since the portfolio value is below the bond-floor. This is called gap risk (see Figure 9.1). The gap at maturity is equal to $(N - V_T)^+$. One of the aims of the model is to calculate the gap risk or, in other words, the present value of these gaps.

We assume the following correlated VG dynamics for the spreads, as in Chapter 8:

$$S_t^{(1)} = S_0^{(\text{iTraxxMain})} \exp(\omega_1 t + \theta_1 G_t + \sigma_1 W_{G_t}^{(1)})$$

$$S_t^{(2)} = S_0^{(\text{iTraxxHiVol})} \exp(\omega_2 t + \theta_2 G_t + \sigma_2 W_{G_t}^{(2)})$$

$$S_t^{(3)} = S_0^{(\text{CDXMain})} \exp(\omega_3 t + \theta_3 G_t + \sigma_3 W_{G_t}^{(3)})$$

$$S_t^{(4)} = S_0^{(\text{CDXHiVol})} \exp(\omega_4 t + \theta_4 G_t + \sigma_4 W_{G_t}^{(4)}),$$

where G_t is a common Gamma process, such that $G_t \sim \text{Gamma}(t/v, 1/v)$, and $W_t^{(i)}$ are correlated standard Brownian motions with a given correlation matrix $\rho^W = (\rho_{ij}^W)$.

We first perform a joint calibration on swaptions of the individual indices. This determines the parameters v and θ_i and σ_i, $i = 1, \ldots, 4$. Next, we match the historical correlations with ρ_{ij} by setting

$$\rho_{ij}^W = \frac{\rho_{ij}\sqrt{\sigma_i^2 + \theta_i^2 v}\sqrt{\sigma_j^2 + \theta_j^2 v} - \theta_i \theta_j v}{\sigma_i \sigma_j}.$$

Hence we are able to match quite accurately all the individual spread dynamics by correlated jump processes and, moreover, are able to impose a correlation structure completely matching the observed historical correlation.

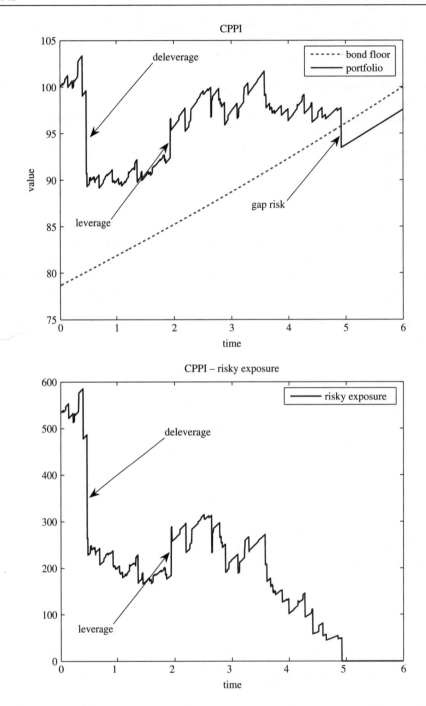

Figure 9.1 CPPI performance, leveraging, deleveraging and gap risk in a multivariate VG driven model

9.3 GAP RISK

Under Black's model (Equation (8.1)) and hypothesizing continuous rebalancing, the gap risk is zero. This happens because of the continuous paths of Brownian motion, which ensures that the bond floor is never crossed but, at worst, is hit, as in Figure 9.2.

One can introduce the gap risk in a Brownian setup via changing the frequency of rebalancing. In Table 9.3, we investigate the impact of such rebalancing frequency. The results are shown for a leveraging factor of $m = 25$ under, respectively, the MVG and Brownian alternatives and $\zeta = 0$. For the MVG case, the parameters are set to the calibrated values; in the Brownian case the volatility σ is set equal for all indices either to 50% (very close to the impled volatility) or to 75%.

In Table 9.3 we give some indicators of the gap risk. More precisely, for different rebalancing frequencies (Rebal), we give the present value of the gap (Risk), the frequency of a gap occurrence (Freq) and the mean size of the gap on condition that there is a gap (Mean). As expected, increasing the rebalancing frequency, decreases the gap frequency and also the size of the gap, given there is a gap. This effect is much more pronounced in the Brownian setting. We further note that the mean return is hardly changing under different rebalancing frequencies. Furthermore, in order, under the Brownian model, to generate gap frequencies of

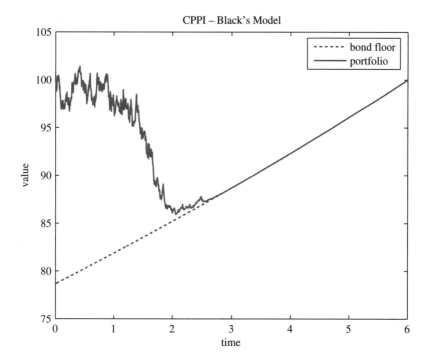

Figure 9.2 The gap risk is zero under Black's model

Table 9.3 Effect of changing the rebalancing frequency of the portfolio under the MVG model and the Black's model

| | **MVG** | | | **BM ($\sigma = 50\%$)** | | | **BM ($\sigma = 75\%$)** | | |
Rebal	Risk	Freq	Mean	Risk	Freq	Mean	Risk	Freq	Mean
2	0.1678	2.34 %	7.17	0.0180	0.73 %	2.50	0.2242	4.77 %	4.70
4	0.1673	2.43 %	6.88	0.0068	0.57 %	1.20	0.0849	3.99 %	2.13
12	0.0942	2.10 %	4.49	0.0005	0.18 %	0.27	0.0067	2.47 %	0.27
52	0.0847	2.10 %	4.04	0.0000	0.02 %	0.00	0.0001	1.02 %	0.01
252	0.0694	2.02 %	3.44	0.0000	0.00 %	0.00	0.0000	0.08 %	0.00

the same magnitude as in the MVG model, one has not only to lower dramatically the rebalancing frequency, but also to increase significantly the volatility used.

The effect of the parameter ζ, or the 'short' positions on the CPPI strategy under MVG is illustrated in Table 9.4. Observe that increasing the amount of shorts from 0% to 100% reduces the return volatility and the portfolio value of the gap risk by almost 50%, while reducing return by only about 5%.

Finally, we investigate the impact of the leverage factor on the return, its volatility and the corresponding gap risk. In Table 9.5, we summarize the results for the MVG model. We observe that increasing the leverage factor, increases significantly the mean return and its volatility, but also the present value of the gap.

Table 9.4 Effect of the parameter ζ, or the 'short' position, on the portfolio strategy under MVG

ζ	Mean of V_T (m EUR)	Std dev (%)	PV gap (m EUR)	Gap (bp p.a.)
0	139.1	11.0	0.0732	1.3720
50%	135.7	8.5	0.0508	0.9531
100%	132.2	6.7	0.0421	0.7892

Table 9.5 Effect of leverage factor under MVG

Leverage m	Mean of V_T (m EUR)	Std (%)	PV gap (m EUR)	Gap (bp p.a.)
25	139.1255	11.0203	0.0732	1.3720
30	141.4980	13.8135	0.1249	2.3405
40	146.2898	19.0518	0.2171	4.0699
50	150.9526	25.4147	0.3609	6.7656

9.4 CPDOs

The Constant Proportion Debt Obligation (CPDO) is another kind of leveraged investment strategy.

The principle behind CPDO is different from the one of the CPPI. In fact, CPDO noteholders do not have a guaranteed capital, but hold a high-rated coupon-bearing note (typically AAA, AA+, ...). Similar to the CPPI case, the CPDO issuers build a portfolio composed of the following instruments:

- the majority of cash is put in risk-free account;
- risky positions are taken by selling protection, e.g., on CDS indices.

The aim of the portfolio strategy is to pay preset coupons (e.g. LIBOR plus 200 bps per annum) during the lifetime of the note; furthermore, at maturity the noteholders get back the notional invested initially.

Once the above target is guaranteed, the risky positions are closed (cash-in event) as is the case in Figure 9.3. If one comes close to the target, one deleverages. If one underperforms, one increases leverage (cfr. a gambler chasing losses). If the portfolio performs badly and falls below a certain low level, we have a cash-out event (cfr. default) as depicted in Figure 9.4.

With respect to the CPPI instrument, the capital guaranteed feature creates a buy at the high and a sell at the low adverse effect. Once losses begin to occur one has to deleverage, decreasing the impact of possible jumps. On the CPDO side, the target return feature means that one buys at the low and sells at the high. Once losses begin to occur one has to leverage more to guarantee the targeted return, possibly creating a very leveraged position, which may increase significantly the

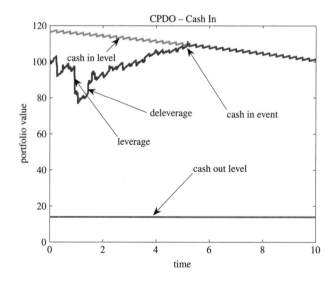

Figure 9.3 CPDO portfolio value evolution and cash-in event

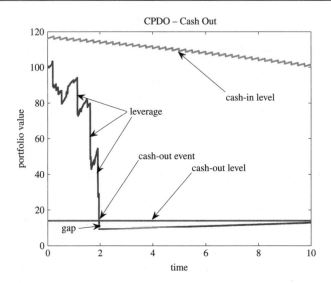

Figure 9.4 CPDO portfolio value evolution and cash-out event

risks due to jumps. As a consequence, one may be more exposed to model risk on a CPDO than on a CPPI.

More precisely, we have the following ingredients and strategy under investigation. We have a prefixed goal, namely an excess return κ, for example, equal to 200 bps per annum over the risk-free rate. In the mechanism, we also fix a target loading factor $\alpha = 1.05$, maximum leverage factor $M = 15$, a cash-out level $C_{out} = 15\%$ and a risky income fraction (fudge factor) $\beta = 0.75$. The fudge factor is typically smaller than 1 in order to compensate for possible defaults or to generate extra margin for the issuer. At each rebalancing date, the CPDO strategy goes as follows:

- Calculate the portfolio value V_t composed out of the cash account, the fee income and the MTM of the positions. Initially, $V_0 = N$, the notional (taken equal to 100 in the figures).
- Calculate the target T_t, which is the present value of all future liabilities, namely the CPDO coupons and the par value of the principal amount.
- If $V_t \geq T_t$, i.e. the portfolio value is above the target, all positions are closed and we have a cash-in.
- If $V_t \leq V_0 \times C_{out}$, i.e. the portfolio value is below the cash-out level, we have a cash-out, all positions are closed and we have a gap of $V_0 \times C_{out} - V_t$.
- If $V_0 \times C_{out} < V_t < T_t$, the portfolio needs to be rebalanced, adjusting risky positions according to the portfolio performance.

In the latter case, the following variables are considered to adjust the leverage:

- The shortfall F_t, i.e. the capital missing to reach the target, is the target-loading factor multiplied by the target minus the portfolio value: $F_t = \alpha T_t - V_t$.

- The present value of the risky income is the fudge factor times the index spread times the risky annuity: $I_t = \beta s_t \times A(0, t)$. If we invest in more underliers, the present value of the risky income is $I_t = \beta \sum_i w_i \times s_t^{(i)} A^{(i)}(0, t)$, where w_i is the weight of the ith underlier, $s_t^{(i)}$ is its spread and $A^{(i)}(0, t)$ is its risky annuity.
- The risky exposure is $E_t = \min \{F_t/I_t, MV_0\}$. Note that under this strategy, the leverage $m = E_t/V_0$ is capped at M.

The first CPDO deal, issued in 2006 by ABN–AMRO, was paying LIBOR plus 200 bps per annum and was rated AAA. A few months later, Moody's released a comment to the effect that, while still standing by their original rating, they acknowledged that it was highly volatile compared to other AAA-rated instruments. This first ever CPDO hit its cash-out trigger in October 2008. Noteholders officially had 10 cents on the dollar at cash-out.

In the following example we hypothesize that the CPDO synthetic portfolio takes a risky position by selling protection on the iTraxx Main and the CDX Main and that $w_1 = w_2 = 1/2$. Imagine that the CPDO has a target return of LIBOR plus 200 bps per annum and that it is rated AAA. Assuming target probabilities for different rating classes on the 10-year horizon as in Table 9.6, this would mean that a return of at least LIBOR plus 200 bps per annum (cash-in) should be achieved in at least 99.27% of the cases.

Under the multivariate VG spread model, calibrated on the index swaptions and with a correlation structure matching historical correlation, we calculate with a Monte-Carlo exercise the cash-in and cash-out probabilities of the CPDO. Given the cash-in probabilities, we can assign a rating to the CPDO by making use of the ratings of Table 9.6. Results for the multivariate VG model are given in Table 9.7; we also give the ratings under a multivariate Brownian (MB) motion setting (which is actually a special case of the MVG setting and corresponds to $\nu \to 0$) for different volatility regimes ($\sigma = 35\%$ and $\sigma = 50\%$).

One observes that the rating is of course dependent on the target return. Moreover, in all the cases the CPDO rating under MVG is lower or equal than under the Brownian models. Additionally, cash-in probabilities under MVG are decreasing faster than under the Brownian models, when one increases the target return. This is caused by the jumps present in the MVG model in combination with the underlying heavier tails incorporated. Also observe that a higher fudge factor implies a higher rating.

The cash-in-time distribution properties for LIBOR + 150 bps per annum for fudge factor $\beta = 75\%$ and $\beta = 100\%$ are graphed in Figure 9.5. Although perhaps at first sight counterintuitive, a lower fudge factor results in a mean cash-in time

Table 9.6 Target probabilities

Rating	AAA	AA+	AA	AA−	A+	A	A−	BBB+
10 years	99.27%	98.99%	98.51%	98.12%	97.71%	97.27%	96.44%	95.22%

Table 9.7 Cash-in probabilities and corresponding ratings for CPDO models as a function of the excess rating

	$\beta = 1$		
Excess return	MVG	$B(\sigma = 35\%)$	$B(\sigma = 50\%)$
100	99.75% (AAA)	99.96% (AAA)	99.87% (AAA)
150	99.44% (AAA)	99.93% (AAA)	99.47% (AAA)
200	98.86% (AA)	99.65% (AAA)	99.30% (AAA)
	$\beta = 0.75$		
	MVG	B_{35}	B_{50}
100	99.02% (AA+)	99.79% (AAA)	99.24% (AA+)
150	97.86% (A+)	99.29% (AAA)	98.35% (AA−)
200	97.43% (A)	98.53% (AA)	97.62% (A)

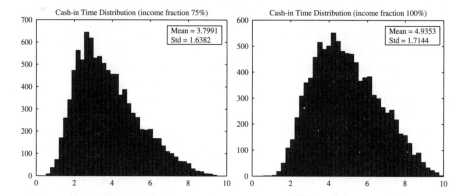

Figure 9.5 Cash-in time distribution for $\beta = 0.75$ and $\beta = 1.00$

that is earlier. The explanation is that a lower fudge factor forces one to increase the leveraged exposure, which often leads to an earlier cash-in time.

Finally, we want to note that the model is not restricted to a credit setting, but you can pimp the model to a hybrid setting. One can set up multivariate Lévy dynamics where, for example, equity indices and stock dynamics are combined with credit dynamics. This is possible where fast vanilla pricers are available for the underlyers, as is the case for equity vanillas and credit swaptions. Hybrid CPPIs or other portfolio products, like CPDOs, taking positions in equity, hedge funds, volatility and credit can be defined and priced.

10

Asset-Backed Securities

10.1   INTRODUCTION

Securitization is the process whereby an institution packs and sells a number of financial assets to a special entity, created specifically for this purpose and therefore termed the Special Purpose Entity (SPE) or Special Purpose Vehicle (SPV), which funds this purchase by issuing notes secured by the revenues from the underlying pool of assets. This form of structured finance was initially developed by the US banking world in the early 1980s (in Mortgage-Backed-Securities (MBSs) format) in order to reduce regulatory capital requirements by removing and transferring risk from the balance sheet to other parties. Over the years, however, the technique has spread to many other industries (also outside the US), with the incentive shifting from reducing capital requirements to funding and hedging. Today, virtually any form of debt obligations and receivables has been securitized, with companies showing a seemingly infinite creativity in allocating the revenues from the pool to the noteholders (respecting their seniority).

Unlike the present very popular Credit Default Swaps, Asset-Backed Securities (ABSs) and MBS contracts are not yet standardized. This lack of uniformity implies that each deal requires a new model. However, there are certain features that emerge in virtually any ABS deal, the most important of which are default risk, amortization of principal value (and thus prepayment risk) and Loss-Given-Default (LGD). Since defaults, losses and accelerated principal repayments can substantially alter the projected cash flows and therefore the planned investment horizon, it is of key importance to adequately describe and model these phenomena when pricing securitization deals.

In some rudimentary ABS models, the probability of default over time is, for example, modelled by means of a (deterministic) logistic function or Vasicek's one-factor model, whereas the prepayment rate and the LGD rate are assumed to be constant (or at least deterministic) over time and independent of default. However, it is intuitively clear that each of these events is coming unexpectedly and is generally driven by the overall economy, hence infecting many borrowers at the same time, causing jumps in the default and prepayment term structures. Therefore it is essential to model the latter by stochastic processes that include jumps. Furthermore, it is unrealistic to assume that prepayment rates and loss rates are time independent and uncorrelated, neither with each other, nor with default rates. For instance, a huge economic downturn will most likely result in a large number of defaults and a decrease in prepayments. Reality indeed shows a negative correlation between default and prepayment.

In this chapter, we propose a number of alternative techniques that can be applied to stochastic models of default and prepayment. The models we propose are based on Lévy processes. In the following section we present four models for the default term structure. In Section 10.3 we discuss three models for the prepayment term structure. Numerical results are presented in Section 10.4, where the default and prepayment models are built into a cash flow model in order to determine the rating and Weighted Average Life (WAL) of two subordinated notes of a simple example ABS deal.

Some general textbook on the topic as well on basic models are Raynes and Rutledge (2003) and Nowell (2008).

10.2 DEFAULT MODELS

In this section we will briefly discuss four models for the default term structure, respectively based on

(1) the Logistic function;
(2) a Lévy portfolio default model;
(3) the Normal one-factor model;
(4) the generic one-factor Lévy model (see, for example, Albrecher *et al.* 2007), with an underlying Shifted Gamma process.

We will focus on the time interval between the issue ($t = 0$) of the ABS notes and the weighted average time to maturity ($t = T$) of the underlying assets. In the following we will use the term *default curve*, $P_d(t)$, to refer to the default term structure, i.e the cumulative default rate at time t. By *default distribution*, we mean the distribution of the cumulative default rate at time T. Hence, the endpoint of the default curve, $P_d(t)$, is a drawing from the default distribution. In this chapter, time is indicated in months: a 10-year ABS deal thus ends at $T = 120$.

10.2.1 Generalized Logistic Default Model

Traditional methods sometimes use a sigmoid (S-shaped) function to model the term structure of defaults, i.e. the default curve. A famous example of such a sigmoid function is the (generalized) Logistic function (see Richards 1959), defined as

$$F(t) = \frac{a}{1 + b\,e^{-c(t-t_0)}}, \tag{10.1}$$

where $F(t)$ satisfies the following ODE

$$\frac{dF(t)}{dt} = c\left(1 - \frac{F(t)}{a}\right)F(t), \tag{10.2}$$

with $b, c, t_0 > 0$, $0 \le a \le 1$ being constants and $t \in [0, T]$.

In the context of default curve modelling, $P_d(t) := F(t)$. Note that when $b = 1$, t_0 corresponds to the inflection point in the loss buildup, i.e. P_d grows at an increasing rate before time t_0 and at a decreasing rate afterwards. Furthermore, $\lim_{t \to +\infty} F(t) = a$, thus a controls the right endpoint of the default curve. For sufficiently large T we can therefore approximate the cumulative default rate at maturity by a, i.e. $P_d(T) \approx a$. Hence, a can be seen as a random draw from a predetermined default distribution (e.g. a truncated Lognormal distribution) and each different value for a will give rise to a new default curve. This makes the Logistic function suitable for scenario analysis. The parameter c determines the growth rate of the Logistic curve, i.e. the proportional increase in one unit of time, as can be seen from Equation (10.2). Values of c between 0.10 and 0.20 produce realistic default curves.

The left panel of Figure 10.1 shows five default curves, generated by the Logistic function with parameters $b = 1, c = 0.1, t_0 = 55$, $T = 120$ and values of a, drawn from a Lognormal distribution with mean 0.20 and standard deviation 0.10. Notice the apparent inflection in the default curve at $t = 55$. The probability density function of the cumulative default rate at time T is shown on the right. Note that theoretically (although with very small probability), the Lognormal distribution with the above given parameters could sample values (for a) above 1. So one should actually work with a truncated version.

It has also to be mentioned that the Logistic function (10.1) has several other drawbacks when it comes to modelling a default curve. First of all, assuming real values for the parameters, the Logistic function does not start at 0, i.e. $P_d(0) > 0$. Moreover, a is only an approximation of the cumulative default rate at maturity, but in general we have that $P_d(T) < a$. Hence P_d has to be rescaled, in order to guarantee that a is indeed the cumulative default rate in the interval $[0, T]$. Secondly, the Logistic function is a deterministic function of time (the only source of randomness is in the choice of the endpoint), whereas defaults generally come as a surprise. And finally, the Logistic function is continuous and hence unable to deal with the shock-driven behaviour of defaults.

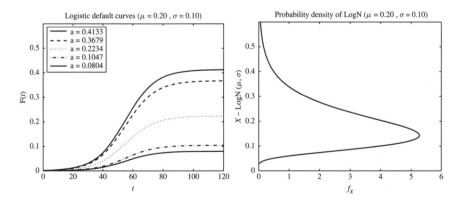

Figure 10.1 Logistic default curve (left) and Lognormal default distribution (right)

In the following subsections, we will describe three default models that (partly) solve the above-mentioned problems. We will use a stochastic (instead of deterministic) process that starts at 0; the shocks will be captured by introducing jumps in the model.

10.2.2 Lévy Portfolio Default Model

The logistic default curve of the previous section does not take into account shocks in the portfolio, i.e. situations where suddenly a significant number of underliers default. We therefore propose a model where the default curve is stochastic and can exhibit a jump behaviour over time. We propose a stochastic default curve model of the form:

$$P_d(t) = 1 - \exp(-\lambda_t^d),$$

where $\lambda^d = \{\lambda_t^d : t \geq 0\}$, is a non-decreasing process starting at zero. The model is based on the classical intensity model framework thinking of Chapter 5 but now applied to a portfolio level and first described in Jönsson et al. (2009).

Here, we assume that λ^d follows a non-decreasing Lévy process and work out the details for the Gamma process $G = \{G_t : t \geq 0\}$, i.e. a Lévy process with Gamma distributed increments, hence

$$\lambda_0^d = 0;$$

$$\lambda_t^d \sim \text{Gamma}(at, b),$$

with shape parameter a and scale parameter b.

From the previous paragraphs it is clear that the cumulative default rate at maturity follows the law of $1 - \exp(-\lambda_T^d)$, where $\lambda_T^d \sim \text{Gamma}(aT, b)$. For predetermined values of the mean μ_d and standard deviation σ_d of the default distribution, one can use this result to find corresponding a and b parameters as the solution to the following system of equations

$$
\begin{aligned}
\mathbb{E}[1 - \exp(-\lambda_T^d)] &= \mu_d; \\
\text{Var}[1 - \exp(-\lambda_T^d)] &= \sigma_d^2.
\end{aligned}
\tag{10.3}
$$

Explicit expressions for the left-hand sides of (10.3) can be found by noting that the expected value and the variance can be written in terms of the characteristic function of the Gamma distribution.

The left panel of Figure 10.2 shows five default curves, generated by Gamma processes with parameters $a \approx 0.024914$, $b \approx 12.904475$ and $T = 120$, such that the mean and standard deviation of the default distribution are $\mu_d = 0.20$ and $\sigma_d = 0.10$. Note that all curves start at zero, include jumps and are fully stochastic functions of time, in the sense that in order to construct a new default curve,

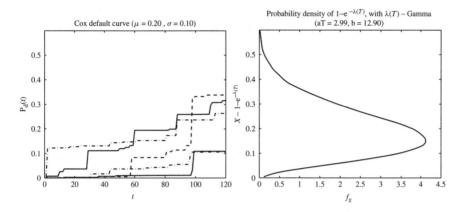

Figure 10.2 Lévy portfolio default curve (left) and corresponding default distribution (right)

one has to rebuild the process λ^d over $[0, T]$, instead of just changing its end-point. The corresponding default probability density function is again shown on the right. Recall, in this case, that $P_d(T)$ follows the law $1 - \exp(-\lambda^d_T)$, with $\lambda^d_T \sim \text{Gamma}(aT, b)$.

10.2.3 Normal One-Factor Default Model

As in the CDO model, we apply here the Normal one-factor (structural) model (Vasicek 1987, Li 1995). Each loan or underlying in the portfolio is described by a latent variable of the form:

$$Z_i = \sqrt{\rho}\, X + \sqrt{1 - \rho}\, X_i, \tag{10.4}$$

with X and $X_i, i = 1, 2, \ldots, N$, identically and independently distributed (i.i.d.) standard Normal variables. As demonstrated in Section 7.2, $\rho = \text{Corr}[Z_i, Z_j]$, for all $i \neq j$. The latter parameter is calibrated to match a predetermined value for the standard deviation σ_d of the default distribution.

A borrower is said to default at time t if its latent variable Z_i is below some (deterministic, but depending on t) barrier K^d_t. The latter default barrier is chosen such that the probability of default before time t matches a predescribed default probabilities. Here, we always assume that default will occur after an exponentially distributed time (cfr. the intensity model driven by a homogeneous Poisson process as in Section 5.1.1) with intensity $\lambda > 0$, i.e. K^d_t satisfies

$$\mathbb{P}(Z_i \leq K^d_t) = \Phi(K^d_t) = 1 - \exp(-\lambda t), \tag{10.5}$$

where Φ denotes, as usual, the standard Normal cumulative distribution function.

Therefore, λ is set such that $\mathbb{P}[Z_i \leq K_T^d] = \mu_d$, with μ_d the predetermined value for the mean of the default distribution. From (10.5) it then follows that

$$\lambda = -\log\left([1 - \mu_d]^{\frac{1}{T}}\right) \tag{10.6}$$

and hence

$$K_t^d = \Phi^{[-1]}\left[1 - (1 - \mu_d)^{\frac{t}{T}}\right]. \tag{10.7}$$

Given a sample of (correlated) standard Normal random variables $\mathbf{Z} = (Z_1, Z_2, \ldots, Z_N)$, the default curve is then given by

$$P_d(t; \mathbf{Z}) = \frac{\sharp\{Z_i \leq K_t^d; \ i = 1, 2, \ldots, N\}}{N}, \ t \geq 0, \tag{10.8}$$

where $\sharp$ indicates that we are counting the number of obligors defaulted at time t.

In order to simulate default curves, one must thus first generate a sample of standard Normal random variables Z_i satisfying (10.4), and then, at each (discrete) time t, count the number of Z_i's that are less than or equal to the value of the default barrier K_t^d at that time.

The left panel of Figure 10.3 shows five default curves, generated by the Normal one-factor model (10.4) with $\rho \approx 0.121353$, such that the mean and standard deviation of the default distribution are $\mu_d = 0.20$ and $\sigma_d = 0.10$ respectively. All curves start at zero and are fully stochastic but, unlike the Lévy portfolio default model, the Normal one-factor default model does not really include any jump dynamics. The corresponding default probability density function is again shown in the right panel.

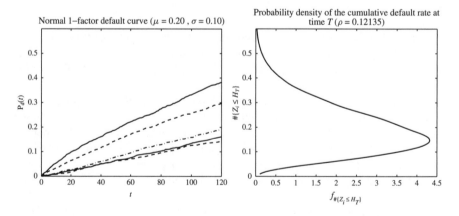

Figure 10.3 Normal one-factor default curve (left) and corresponding default distribution (right)

10.2.4   Generic One-Factor Lévy Default Model

As in Chapter 7, one can extend the Normal one-factor model to a more general class based on other multivariate latent variables. Under the generic one-factor Lévy model the latent variable of borrower i is now given by

$$A^{(i)} = Y_\rho + Y_{1-\rho}^{(i)}, \tag{10.9}$$

with Y and $Y^{(i)}$, $i = 1, 2, \ldots, N$, i.i.d. Lévy processes, based on the same mother infinitely divisible distribution L, such that $\mathbb{E}[Y_1] = 0$ and $\mathrm{Var}[Y_1] = 1$, which implies that $\mathrm{Var}[Y_t] = t$. From this it is clear that $\mathbb{E}[A^{(i)}] = 0$ and $\mathrm{Var}[A^{(i)}] = 1$, and that $\mathrm{Corr}[A^{(i)}, A^{(j)}] = \rho$, for all $i \neq j$. As with the Normal one-factor model, the cross-correlation ρ will be calibrated to match a predetermined standard deviation for the default distribution.

Similar to the Normal one-factor model, we again say that a borrower defaults at time t if $A^{(i)}$ is below a predetermined barrier K_t^d at that time, where K_t^d satisfies

$$\mathbb{P}\left(A^{(i)} \leq K_t^d\right) = 1 - \exp(-\lambda t), \tag{10.10}$$

with λ given by (10.6).

Here, we illustrate the theory by assuming that Y and $Y^{(i)}$, $i = 1, 2, \ldots, N$, are i.i.d. Shifted Gamma processes, i.e. $Y = \{Y_t = t\tilde{\mu} - G_t, t \geq 0\}$, where G is a Gamma process, with shape parameter a and scale parameter b. From (10.9) and the fact that a Gamma distribution is infinitely divisible, it follows that

$$A^{(i)} \stackrel{d}{=} \tilde{\mu} - \tilde{X} \stackrel{d}{=} \tilde{\mu} - [X + X_i], \tag{10.11}$$

with $X \sim \mathrm{Gamma}(a\rho, b)$ and $X_i \sim \mathrm{Gamma}(a(1 - \rho), b)$ mutually independent and $\tilde{X} \sim \mathrm{Gamma}(a, b)$. The symbol $\stackrel{d}{=}$ denotes that the variables are equal in distribution. If we take $\tilde{\mu} = \frac{a}{b}$ and $b = \sqrt{a}$, we ensure that $\mathbb{E}[A^{(i)}] = 0$, $\mathrm{Var}[A^{(i)}] = 1$ and $\mathrm{Corr}[A^{(i)}, A^{(j)}] = \rho$, for all $i \neq j$.

Furthermore, from (10.10), (10.11) and the expression for λ it follows that

$$K_t^d = \tilde{\mu} - \Gamma_{a,b}^{[-1]}\left((1 - \mu_d)^{\frac{t}{T}}\right), \tag{10.12}$$

where $\Gamma_{a,b}^{[-1]}$ denotes the inverse of the cumulative distribution function of a $\mathrm{Gamma}(a, b)$ distribution.

In order to simulate default curves, we first have to generate a sample of random variables $\mathbf{A} = (A^{(1)}, A^{(2)}, \ldots, A^{(N)})$ satisfying (10.9), with $Y, Y^{(1)}, Y^{(2)}, \ldots, Y^{(N)}$, i.i.d. Shifted Gamma processes and then, at each (discrete) time t, count the number of $A^{(i)}$'s that are lower than or equal to the value of the default barrier K_t^d at that time. Hence, the default curve is given by

$$P_d(t; \mathbf{A}) = \frac{\#\{A^{(i)} \leq K_t^d; \ i = 1, 2, \ldots, N\}}{N}, \quad t \geq 0. \tag{10.13}$$

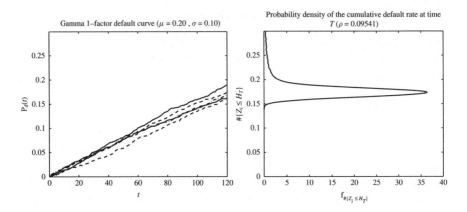

Figure 10.4 Gamma one-factor default curve (left) and corresponding default distribution (right)

The left panel of Figure 10.4 shows five default curves, generated by the Gamma one-factor model (10.9) with $(\tilde{\mu}, a, b) = (1, 1, 1)$, and $\rho \approx 0.095408$, such that the mean and standard deviation of the default distribution are 0.20 and 0.10. Again, all curves start at zero and are fully stochastic. The corresponding default probability density function is shown in the right panel. Compared to the previous three default models, the default probability density function generated by the Shifted Gamma-Lévy model seems to be more peaked around μ_d and has a significantly larger kurtosis. The default distribution has a rather heavy right tail, with a substantial probability mass at the 100% default rate. This can be explained by looking at the right-hand side of Equation (10.11). Since both terms between brackets are strictly positive and hence cannot compensate each other (unlike the Normal one-factor model), $A^{(i)}$ is bounded from above by $\tilde{\mu}$. Hence, starting with a large systematic risk factor X, things can only get worse, i.e. the term between brackets can only increase and therefore $A^{(i)}$ can only result in a lower value when adding the idiosyncratic risk factor X_i. This implies that when we have a substantially large common factor (close to $\Gamma_{a,b}^{[-1]}(1 - \mu_d)$, cfr. (10.12)), it is very likely that all borrowers will default, i.e. that $A^{(i)} \leq K_T^d$ for all $i = 1, 2, \ldots, N$.

10.3 PREPAYMENT MODELS

In this section we will briefly discuss three models for the prepayment term structure, respectively based on

(1) constant prepayment;
(2) Lévy portfolio prepayment model;
(3) the Normal one-factor model.

As before, we will use the terms *prepayment curve*, $P_p(t)$, $0 \leq t \leq T$ and *prepayment distribution* to refer to the prepayment term structure and the distribution of the cumulative prepayment rate at maturity T.

10.3.1 Constant Prepayment Model

The idea of constant prepayment stems from the former Public Securities Association[1] (PSA). The basic assumption is that prepayment intensity begins at 0 and rises at a constant rate of increase α, until it reaches its characteristic steady-state rate at time τ_0, after which the prepayment rate remains constant until maturity T. Note that τ_0 is generally not the same as the inflection point t_0 of the default curve.

Thus the prepayment intensity, cpr, and the cumulative prepayment curves CPR (the integral of the intensity rate) are given by

$$
\mathrm{cpr}(t) = \begin{cases} \alpha t; & 0 \leq t \leq \tau_0 \\ \alpha \tau_0; & \tau_0 \leq t \leq T \end{cases}
\tag{10.14}
$$

and

$$
\mathrm{CPR}(t) = \begin{cases} \frac{\alpha t^2}{2}; & 0 \leq t \leq \tau_0 \\ -\frac{\alpha \tau_0^2}{2} + \alpha \tau_0 t; & \tau_0 \leq t \leq T \end{cases}
\tag{10.15}
$$

The constant prepayment model takes $P_p(t) = \mathrm{CPR}(t)$.

From (10.14) it is obvious that the prepayment rate increases at a speed of α per period before time τ_0 and remains constant afterwards. Consequently, the cumulative prepayment curve (10.15) increases quadratically on the interval $[0, \tau_0]$ and linearly on $[\tau_0, T]$. Given τ_0 and $P_p(T) = \mathrm{CPR}(T)$, i.e. the cumulative prepayment rate at maturity, the constant rate of increase α equals

$$
\alpha = \frac{\mathrm{CPR}(T)}{T\tau_0 - \frac{\tau_0^2}{2}}.
\tag{10.16}
$$

Hence, once τ_0 and $\mathrm{CPR}(T)$ are fixed, the marginal and cumulative prepayment curves are completely deterministic. Moreover, the CPR model does not include jumps. Due to these features, the CPR model is an unrealistic representation of real-life prepayments, which are shock-driven and typically show some random effects. In the following sections we will describe two models that (partially) solve these problems.

Figure 10.5 shows the marginal and cumulative prepayment curve when the steady state τ_0 is reached after 18 months and the cumulative prepayment rate at maturity equals $P_p(5) = \mathrm{CPR}(5) = 0.20$.

---

[1] In 1997 the PSA changed its name to The Bond Market Association (TBMA), which merged with the Securities Industry Association on 1 November 2006, to form the Securities Industry and Financial Markets Association (SIFMA).

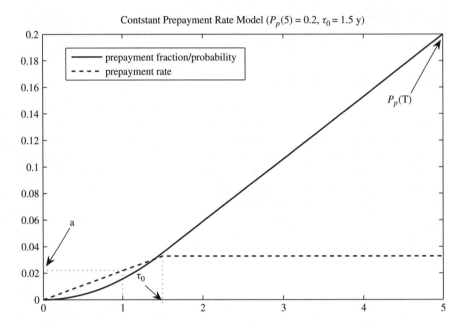

Figure 10.5 Marginal and cumulative constant prepayment curve: $CPR(5) = P_p(5) = 0.20$, $\tau_0 = 1.5$ years

10.3.2 Lévy Portfolio Prepayment Model

The Lévy portfolio prepayment model is completely analogous to the Lévy portfolio default model described in Section 10.2.2. We propose a stochastic prepayment curve model of the form:

$$P_p(t) = 1 - \exp(-\lambda_t^p),$$

where $\lambda^p = \{\lambda_t^p, t \geq 0\}$, is a non-decreasing process starting at zero. The model is again based on the classical intensity model framework thinking of Chapter 5, but now applied to a portfolio level. In the example, we again make use of a Gamma process for λ^p.

10.3.3 Normal One-Factor Prepayment Model

The Normal one-factor prepayment model starts from the same underlying philosophy as its default equivalent of Section 10.2.3. We again use the latent variable setting, but now include prepayment. The ith borrower prepays at the time t, the first time Z_i is *above* a prespecified upper bound K_t^p.

The barrier K_t^p is chosen such that the expected probability of prepayment before time t equals the (observed) cumulative prepayment curve $CPR(t)$, given by (10.15), i.e.

$$\mathbb{P}(Z_i \geq K_t^p) = 1 - \Phi(K_t^p) = \text{CPR}(t), \tag{10.17}$$

which implies that

$$K_t^p = \Phi^{[-1]}(1 - \text{CPR}(t)), \tag{10.18}$$

with $\Phi^{[-1]}$, as before, the inverse of the standard Normal cumulative distribution function.

In order to simulate prepayment curves, we must thus draw a sample standard Normal random variable $\mathbf{Z} = (Z_1, Z_2, \ldots, Z_N)$ satisfying (10.1), and then, at each (discrete) time t, count the number of Z_i's that are greater than or equal to the value of the prepayment barrier H_t^p at that time. The prepayment curve is then given by

$$P_p(t; \mathbf{Z}) = \frac{\sharp\{Z_i \geq K_t^p : i = 1, 2, \ldots, N\}}{N}, \quad t \geq 0. \tag{10.19}$$

The left panel of Figure 10.6 shows five prepayment curves, generated by the Normal one-factor model (10.4) with $\rho \approx 0.121353$, such that the mean and standard deviation of the prepayment distribution are 0.20 and 0.10 (as for the default model). The fact that the cross-correlation coefficient ρ is the same as the one of the default model is a direct consequence of the symmetry of the Normal distribution. The corresponding prepayment probability density function is shown in the right panel.

We note finally that other one-factor Lévy models can also be set up in the same spirit. However, in order to have some realism, these should be based upon

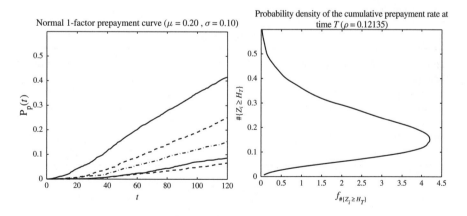

Figure 10.6 Normal one-factor prepayment curve (left) and corresponding prepayment distribution (right)

a two-side distribution (the real line). Hence the Shifted Gamma model is not considered here because of the upper endpoint ($\tilde{\mu}$).

10.4 NUMERICAL RESULTS

One can now build these default and prepayment models into any scenario generator for pricing, rating and determining the Weighted Average Life (WAL) of notes backed by an underlying asset pool. Any combination of the above described default and prepayment models is possible, except for the combination of the generic one-factor Lévy default model with the Normal one-factor prepayment model. Otherwise the borrower's cash position would be modelled by two different processes: one to obtain his default probability and another for his prepayment probability, which is neither consistent nor realistic.

Hence, we consider 11 different scenario generators.

We will now apply each of the above-mentioned 11 default–prepayment combinations to derive the expected loss and the corresponding rating and WAL of two (subordinated) notes backed by a pool of commercial loans. Table 10.1 lists the specifications of the ABS deal under consideration.

Table 10.1 Specifications of the ABS deal

ASSETS		
Initial balance of the asset pool	V_0	$30,000,000
Number of loans in the asset pool	N_0	2,000
Weighted Average Maturity of the assets	WAM	10 years
Weighted Average Coupon of the assets	WAC	12% p.a.
Payment frequency		monthly
Reserve target		5%
interest rate on reserve account		3.92% p.a.
Loss-Given-Default	LGD	50%
LIABILITIES		
Initial balance of the senior note	A_0	$24,000,000
Premium of the senior note	r_A	7% p.a.
Initial balance of the subordinated note	B_0	$6,000,000
Premium of the subordinated note	r_B	9% p.a.
Servicing fee	r_{sf}	1% p.a.
Shortfall fee	r_{sh}	20% p.a.
Payment method		Pro-rata

The so-called *waterfall structure* of this example ABS deal works as follows. Each month some cash is collected. This cash can come from four sources: interest payments of the underlying loans, unscheduled prepayment of loans (modelled by the above prepayment curves), recovery values in case of defaults (modelled by the above default curves) and the scheduled principle repayments. The collected amount is then redistributed according to the following rules:

1. First, a *servicing fee* of r_{sf} on the outstanding balance of the asset pool, say V_t, is paid out to the SPV. Note that the initial outstanding balance is V_0, but that this value is decreasing over time because of redemptions, prepayments and defaults.
2. Next, the interest r_A on the outstanding balance of Note A in the beginning of the collection period (A_t) is paid out to the Note A holders. Note that the initial outstanding balance of Note A is A_0, but that this value again is decreasing over time because of redemptions.
3. Then, the interest r_B on the outstanding balance of Note B in the beginning of the collection period (B_t) is paid out to the Note B holders. Same remark as above holds on the initial outstanding balance of Note B, B_0 and its decrease over time.
4. Next, the scheduled principal redemption of Note A is paid out.
5. Finally, the scheduled principal redemption of Note B is paid out.

The amount that is left over is put on a *reserve account*. The reserve account has an upper limit which is a fixed percentage (in our example 5% p.a.) of the outstanding balance of the asset pool at the end of the collection period. Any excess cash goes to the owners of the SPV. If, for a certain month, in the above waterfall structure, one has not enough money, one uses the money in the reserve account to honour its obligations. If there is no longer any money in the reserve account, payments are postponed to the next month. However, each month the waterfall sequences is respected. So, if in a certain month, one cannot honour the third step (and the following ones) in the waterfall, next month's money is used first to pay out steps 1 and 2 and then one is paying for steps 3, 4 and 5. One is then paying last month's obligations and this month's obligations. However, on the servicing fee payments that were not paid out on time, an extra shortfall fee r_{sh} is added. As the servicing fee is accrued with this shortfall fee, the overdue interest rate payments are accrued with the respective premiums r_A and r_B.

In the above waterfall, we have a so-called *pro-rata redemption* of principal, which means that in each month part of the outstanding balance of Note A *and*

Table 10.2 Some important parameters

Mean of the default distribution	μ_d	20%
Standard deviation of the default distribution	σ_d	10%
Mean of the prepayment distribution	μ_p	20%
Standard deviation of the prepayment distribution	σ_p	10%
Parameters of the Logistic curve	b	1
	c	0.1
	t_0	55 months
Steady state of the prepayment curve	τ_0	45 months

Note B is supposed to be redeemed. Another popular mechanism is the so-called *sequential redemption*, where first the total outstanding balance of Note A is paid back and then one starts with redeeming Note B holders.

It should be noted that this is just an example. Each ABS deal is different. There can be different notes/tranches, with different outstanding balances, the priority rules (in the waterfall) of the payments can be different, the existence of and the functioning of the reserve account can change, other redemption mechanisms can be in place, etc.

The reserve account can be seen as a credit enhancement instrument, as is illustrated in Table 10.5. Other types of insurance are of course possible.

We will use the parameter values mentioned in Table 10.2 to rate the above described deal under the different models.

Tables 10.3 and 10.4 contain the ratings (based on the Moody's Idealized Cumulative Expected Loss Rates, cfr. Cifuentes and O'Connor 1996) and the difference between the promised and the realized return (DIRR) and WALs of the two ABS notes, obtained with each of the 11 default–prepayment combinations and for several choices of μ_d, and μ_p. The figures presented in these tables are averages based on a Monte Carlo simulation with a million scenarios. To be precise, a rating is determined in the following way. We first look at the WAL and (by interpolation) calculate for each rating class the corresponding cumulative Expected Loss rates, then we compare these with the Monte Carlo calculated DIRR.

The WAL is defined as

$$\text{WAL} = \frac{1}{P}\left(\sum_{t=1}^{T} t \cdot P_t + T\left[P - \sum_{t=1}^{T} P_t\right]\right), \tag{10.20}$$

where P_t is the total principal paid at time t and P is the initial balance of the note.

More specifically, in Table 10.3 we investigate what happens to the ratings if μ_d is changed, while holding μ_p and σ_p constant,[2] whereas Table 10.4 provides insight in the impact of a change in μ_p, while keeping μ_d and σ_d fixed.

---

[2] In order to keep μ_p and σ_p fixed, also the cross-correlation ρ must remain fixed, since there is a unique parameter ρ for each pair (μ_p, σ_p) (or equivalently (μ_d, σ_d)). This also explains why σ_d changes if μ_d changes.

Table 10.3 Ratings, DIRR and WAL of the ABS notes, for different combinations of default and prepayment models and mean cumulative default rate $\mu_d = 0.10, 0.20, 0.40$ and mean cumulative prepayment rate $\mu_p = 0.20$

Note A

Model pair	Rating			DIRR (bp)			WAL (year)		
	$\mu_d = 10\%$	$\mu_d = 20\%$	$\mu_d = 40\%$	$\mu_d = 10\%$	$\mu_d = 20\%$	$\mu_d = 40\%$	$\mu_d = 10\%$	$\mu_d = 20\%$	$\mu_d = 40\%$
Logistic – CPR	Aaa	Aa1	Aa3	0.026746	0.3466	5.3712	5.4867	5.2742	4.8642
Logistic – Lévy portfolio	Aaa	Aa1	A1	0.039664	0.48683	7.4258	5.343	5.1311	4.729
Logistic – Normal-1-factor	Aaa	Aa1	Aa3	0.027104	0.3278	5.1148	5.4869	5.2745	4.8656
Lévy portfolio – CPR	Aaa	Aaa	A1	0.0017992	0.16105	9.0857	5.4799	5.2529	4.7895
Lévy portfolio – Lévy portfolio	Aaa	Aaa	A1	0.0067859	0.34616	12.044	5.3355	5.1101	4.6543
Lévy portfolio – Normal-1-factor	Aaa	Aaa	A1	0.0032759	0.20977	9.0265	5.4795	5.2532	4.7912
Normal-1-factor – CPR	Aaa	Aaa	Aa2	0.00036114	0.034631	2.9626	5.4775	5.2427	4.7309
Normal-1-factor – Lévy portfolio	Aaa	Aaa	Aa3	0.00060627	0.055516	3.6883	5.3335	5.0986	4.5895
Normal-1-factor – Normal-1-factor	Aaa	Aaa	Aa2	0.00014211	0.017135	2.0175	5.4774	5.2427	4.7303
Gamma-1-factor – CPR	Aa1	Aa3	A2	1.4443	4.6682	18.431	5.4828	5.2599	4.7939
Gamma-1-factor – Lévy portfolio	Aa2	Aa3	A2	2.5931	4.9614	20.385	5.3427	5.1167	4.6503

Note B

Model pair	Rating			DIRR (bp)			WAL (year)		
	$\mu_d = 10\%$	$\mu_d = 20\%$	$\mu_d = 40\%$	$\mu_d = 10\%$	$\mu_d = 20\%$	$\mu_d = 40\%$	$\mu_d = 10\%$	$\mu_d = 20\%$	$\mu_d = 40\%$
Logistic – CPR	Aa1	A1	Baa3	0.93026	10.581	139.46	5.4901	5.3124	5.3358
Logistic – Lévy portfolio	Aa1	A1	Baa3	1.1996	13.624	164.07	5.3471	5.1771	5.2456
Logistic – Normal-1-factor	Aa1	A1	Baa3	0.93764	10.906	140.55	5.4903	5.3135	5.3391
Lévy portfolio – CPR	Aa1	A2	Baa3	1.4051	17.801	175.75	5.4949	5.3525	5.4753
Lévy portfolio – Lévy portfolio	Aa2	A2	Ba1	1.9445	21.891	195.61	5.3526	5.2204	5.373
Lévy portfolio – Normal-1-factor	Aa1	A2	Baa3	1.6019	18.35	175.49	5.4951	5.353	5.4738
Normal-1-factor – CPR	Aaa	Aa1	Baa1	0.033692	1.5642	57.936	5.4777	5.2502	4.9709
Normal-1-factor – Lévy portfolio	Aaa	Aa2	Baa2	0.041807	1.9829	65.669	5.3337	5.1071	4.8421
Normal-1-factor – Normal-1-factor	Aaa	Aa1	Baa1	0.023184	1.156	48.936	5.4776	5.2491	4.9498
Gamma-1-factor – CPR	Aa3	A2	Baa2	6.288	20.736	85.662	5.4955	5.3022	4.9739
Gamma-1-factor – Lévy portfolio	A1	A3	Baa3	15.293	28.406	120.76	5.3631	5.1588	4.8351

Table 10.4 Ratings, DIRR and WAL of the ABS notes, for different combinations of default and prepayment models and mean cumulative default rate $\mu_d = 0.20$ and mean cumulative prepayment rate $\mu_p = 0.10, 0.20, 0.40$

Note A

Model pair	Rating			DIRR (bp)			WAL (year)		
	$\mu_p = 10\%$	$\mu_p = 20\%$	$\mu_p = 40\%$	$\mu_p = 10\%$	$\mu_p = 20\%$	$\mu_p = 40\%$	$\mu_p = 10\%$	$\mu_p = 20\%$	$\mu_p = 40\%$
Logistic – CPR	Aa1	Aa1	Aa1	0.31365	0.3466	0.27714	5.4309	5.2742	4.9611
Logistic – Lévy portfolio	Aa1	Aa1	Aa1	0.34552	0.48683	0.90665	5.365	5.1311	4.618
Logistic – Normal-1-factor	Aa1	Aa1	Aa1	0.30488	0.3278	0.25706	5.431	5.2745	4.9633
Lévy portfolio – CPR	Aaa	Aaa	Aa1	0.10416	0.16105	0.42327	5.4093	5.2529	4.9404
Lévy portfolio – Lévy portfolio	Aaa	Aa1	Aa1	0.14828	0.34616	1.4266	5.3439	5.1101	4.5982
Lévy portfolio – Normal-1-factor	Aaa	Aa1	Aa1	0.11976	0.20977	0.51304	5.4096	5.2532	4.9424
Normal-1-factor – CPR	Aaa	Aaa	Aaa	0.023787	0.034631	0.046599	5.3995	5.2427	4.9292
Normal-1-factor – Lévy portfolio	Aaa	Aaa	Aaa	0.03208	0.055516	0.1094	5.3335	5.0986	4.5842
Normal-1-factor – Normal-1-factor	Aaa	Aaa	Aaa	0.016874	0.017135	0.018373	5.3995	5.2427	4.9291
Gamma-1-factor – CPR	Aa3	Aa3	Aa2	5.811	4.6682	2.8855	5.4149	5.2599	4.9497
Gamma-1-factor – Lévy portfolio	Aa3	Aa3	Aa2	6.7492	4.9614	3.2188	5.3487	5.1167	4.6043

Note B

Model pair	Rating			DIRR (bp)			WAL (year)		
	$\mu_p = 10\%$	$\mu_p = 20\%$	$\mu_p = 40\%$	$\mu_p = 10\%$	$\mu_p = 20\%$	$\mu_p = 40\%$	$\mu_p = 10\%$	$\mu_p = 20\%$	$\mu_p = 40\%$
Logistic – CPR	A1	A1	A2	8.9089	10.581	14.756	5.4642	5.3124	5.0111
Logistic – Lévy portfolio	A1	A1	A3	9.9097	13.624	26.681	5.4011	5.1771	4.695
Logistic – Normal-1-factor	A1	A1	A2	9.0211	10.906	14.436	5.4646	5.3135	5.0123
Lévy portfolio – CPR	A1	A2	A3	14.216	17.801	27.506	5.4994	5.3525	5.0628
Lévy portfolio – Lévy portfolio	A1	A2	Baa1	15.687	21.891	42.04	5.4384	5.2204	4.7511
Lévy portfolio – Normal-1-factor	A1	A2	A3	14.318	18.35	28.531	5.4992	5.353	5.0644
Normal-1-factor – CPR	Aa1	Aa1	Aa2	1.3334	1.5642	2.0323	5.4064	5.2502	4.9375
Normal-1-factor – Lévy portfolio	Aa1	Aa2	Aa3	1.4404	1.9829	3.4481	5.3406	5.1071	4.5943
Normal-1-factor – Normal-1-factor	Aa1	Aa1	Aa1	1.1397	1.156	1.2153	5.4059	5.2491	4.9356
Gamma-1-factor – CPR	Baa1	A2	A1	54.297	20.736	11.785	5.4614	5.3022	4.9848
Gamma-1-factor – Lévy portfolio	A3	A3	A2	42.16	28.406	17.871	5.3945	5.1588	4.6418

Table 10.5 Ratings, DIRR and WAL of the ABS notes, for different combinations of default and prepayment models with and without reserve account. Mean cumulative default rate $\mu_d = 0.20$ and mean cumulative prepayment rate $\mu_p = 0.20$

Note A

Model pair	Rating		DIRR (bp)		WAL (year)	
	Reserve (PR)	No Reserve (PR)	Reserve (PR)	No Reserve (PR)	Reserve (PR)	No Reserve (PR)
Logistic – CPR	Aa1	Aa1	0.3466	0.71815	5.2742	5.2752
Logistic – Lévy portfolio	Aa1	Aa1	0.48683	1.0068	5.1311	5.1327
Logistic – Normal-1-factor	Aa1	Aa1	0.327	0.7184	5.2745	5.2755
Lévy portfolio – CPR	Aaa	Aa1	0.16105	0.71116	5.2529	5.28
Lévy portfolio – Lévy portfolio	Aa1	Aa1	0.34616	1.1772	5.1101	5.1379
Lévy portfolio – Normal-1-factor	Aa1	Aa1	0.0977	0.80489	5.2532	5.2802
Normal-1-factor – CPR	Aaa	Aaa	0.034631	0.16448	5.2427	5.2437
Normal-1-factor – Lévy portfolio	Aaa	Aa1	0.055516	0.26287	5.0986	5.0997
Normal-1-factor – Normal-1-factor	Aaa	Aaa	0.017135	0.051144	5.2427	5.2437
Gamma-1-factor – CPR	Aa3	Aa3	4.6682	5.9435	5.2599	5.264
Gamma-1-factor – Lévy portfolio	Aa3	Aa3	4.9614	6.5872	5.1167	5.1207

Note B

Model pair	Rating		DIRR (bp)		WAL (year)	
	Reserve (PR)	No Reserve (PR)	Reserve (PR)	No Reserve (PR)	Reserve (PR)	No Reserve (PR)
Logistic – CPR	A1	A3	10.581	38.957	5.3124	5.4739
Logistic – Lévy portfolio	A1	Baa1	13.624	46.316	5.1771	5.3522
Logistic – Normal-1-factor	A1	A3	10.906	39.955	5.3135	5.4763
Lévy portfolio – CPR	A2	Baa1	17.801	67.004	5.3525	5.6466
Lévy portfolio – Lévy portfolio	A2	Baa2	21.891	75.017	5.5204	5.5242
Lévy portfolio – Normal-1-factor	A2	Baa1	18.35	67.608	5.353	5.6467
Normal-1-factor – CPR	Aa1	A1	1.5642	8.5988	5.2502	5.3062
Normal-1-factor – Lévy portfolio	Aa2	A1	1.9829	10.739	5.1071	5.171
Normal-1-factor – Normal-1-factor	Aa1	Aa3	1.156	5.4548	5.2491	5.2995
Gamma-1-factor – CPR	A2	A3	20.736	30.589	5.3022	5.341
Gamma-1-factor – Lévy portfolio	A3	A3	28.406	37.646	5.1588	5.1986

The effect of having no reserve account in the pro-rata case is shown in Table 10.5. For a full sensitivity analysis, we refer to Jönsson *et al.* (2009).

Traditional models for the rating and the analysis of ABSs are typically based on Normal distribution assumptions and Brownian motion-driven dynamics. The Normal distribution belongs to the class of the so-called light-tailed distributions. This means that extreme events, shock, jumps, crashes, etc., are not incorporated in the Normal distribution based models. However looking at empirical data and certainly in the light of the credit crunch financial crisis, these extreme events can have a dramatic impact on the product. Hence, in order to do a better assessment, new models incorporating these features are needed. Having introduced a whole battery of models based on more flexible distributions incorporating extreme events and jumps in the sample paths, we observe an important impact of such models on the (D)IRR and the WAL and consequently on the rating of ABSs.

Bibliography

Albrecher, H., Ladoucette, S. and Schoutens, W. (2007). A generic one-factor Lévy model for pricing synthetic CDOs. In R.J. Elliott *et al.* (eds) *Advances in Mathematical Finance*. Birkhäuser.

Andersen, L., Sidenius, J. and Basu, S. (2003). All your hedges in one basket. *Risk*, **16** (11), 67–72.

Anderson, R. and Sundaresan, S. (1996). Design and valuation of debt contracts. *Review of Financial Studies*, **9**, 37–68.

Appelbaum, D. (2004). *Lévy Processes and Stochastic Calculus*. Cambridge University Press.

Barndorff-Nielsen, O. (2001). Superposition of Ornstein–Uhlenbeck type processes. *Theory of Probability and its Applications*, **45**, 175–194.

Barndorff-Nielsen, O. and Shephard, N. (2001a). Non-Gaussian Ornstein–Uhlenbeck-based models and some of their uses in financial economics. *Journal of the Royal Statistical Society, Series B*, **63**, 167–241.

Barndorff-Nielsen, O. and Shephard, N. (2001b). Modelling by Lévy processes for financial econometrics. In O.E. Barndorff-Nielsen, T. Mikosch and S. Resnick (eds), *Lévy Processes – Theory and Applications*, pp. 283–318.

Barndorff-Nielsen, O. and Shephard, N. (2003). Integrated OU–processes and non-Gaussian OU–based stochastic volatility models. *Scandinavian Journal of Statistics*, **30**, 277–295.

Basel Accord, I. (2004). *International convergence of capital measurement and capital standards*. Tech. Report, Bank for International Settlement.

Baxter, M. (2007). Gamma process dynamic modelling of credit. *Risk Magazine*, October, 98–101.

Bertoin, J. (1996). *Lévy Processes*. Cambridge University Press, Cambridge.

Bertrand, P. and Prigent, J.L. (2002). Portfolio insurance: the extreme value approach to the CPPI method. *Finance*, **23**, 68–86.

Bertrand, P. and Prigent, J.L. (2003). Portfolio insurance strategies: a comparison of standard methods when the volatitlity of the stock is stochastic. *International Journal of Business*, **8** (4), 461–472.

Bertrand, P. and Prigent, J.L. (2005). Portfolio insurance strategies: OBPI versus CPPI. *Finance*, **26** (1), 5–32.

Bielecki, T. (2008). *Rating SME transactions*. Moody's Investors Service.

Bielecki, T. and Rutkowski, M. (2002). *Credit Risk: Modelling, Valuation and Hedging*. Springer Finance, London.

Bingham, N.H. and Kiesel, R. (1998). *Risk-Neutral Valuation. Pricing and Hedging of Financial Derivatives*. Springer Finance, London.

Björk, T. (1998). *Arbitrage Theory in Continous Time*. Oxford University Press Inc., New York.

Black, F. and Cox, J. (1976). Valuing corporate securities: some effects on bond indenture provisions. *Journal of Finance*, **31**, 351–367.

Black, F. and Jones, R. (1987). Simplifying portfolio insurance. *Journal of Portfolio Management*, **31**, 48–51.

Black, F. and Scholes, M. (1973). The pricing of options and corporate liabilities. *Journal of Political Economy*, **81**, 637–654.

Cariboni, J. and Schoutens, W. (2007). Pricing credit default swaps under Lévy models. *Journal of Computational Finance*, **10**.

Carr, P. and Madan, D. (1999). Option valuation using the Fast Fourier Transform. *Journal of Computational Finance*, **2**, 61–73.

Carr, P. and Wu, L. (2003). The finite moment logstable process and option pricing. *Journal of Finance*, **58** (2), 753–778.

Cifuentes, A. and O'Connor, G. (1996). *The binomial expansion method applied to CBO/CLO analysis*. Moody's Special Report.

Cifuentes, A. and Wilcox, C. (1998). *The double binomial method and its application to a special case of CBO structures*. Moody's Special Report.

Clark, P. (1973). A subordinated stochastic process with finite variance for speculative prices. *Econometrica*, **41**, 135–156.

Coffey, M. (2007) LCDS and loan spreads, *LPC Gold Sheets*, **21** (11), 1–24. Reuters Loan Pricing Corporation Publication.

Cont, R. and Tankov, P. (2004). *Financial Modelling with Jump Processes*. Chapman and Hall.

Cont, R. and Tankov, P. (2007). *Constant proportion portfolio insurance in presence of jumps in asset pricess*. SSRN Working Paper Series.

Cox, J., Ingersoll, J. and Ross, S. (1985). A theory of the term structure of interest rates. *Econometrica*, **53**, 385–408.

Das, S. (2000). *Credit Derivatives and Credit Linked Notes*. John Wiley & Sons, Ltd., Chichester.

Devroye, L. (1986). *Non-Uniform Random Variate Generation*. Springer-Verlag, New York.

Dobránszky, P. (2008). *Numerical quadratures to calculate Lévy base correlation*. Technical Report 08-02, Section of Statistics, K.U. Leuven.

Duffie, D., Filipović, D. and Schachermayer, W. (2003). Affine processes and application in finance. *The Annals of Applied Probability*, **13**, 984–1053.

Duffie, D. and Singleton, K. (1999). Modelling term structures of defaultable risky bonds. *Review of Financial Studies*, **12**, 687–720.

Duffie, D. and Singleton, K. (2003). *Credit Risk*. Princeton University Press, Cambridge.

Garcia, J. and Goossens, S. (2007b). *Base expected loss explains Lévy base correlation smile*. Working paper.

Garcia, J. and Goossens, S. (2007a). Explaining the Lévy base correlation smile. *Risk Magazine*, July.

Garcia, J., Goossens, S. and Schoutens, W. (2008). Let's jump together: pricing credit derivatives. *Risk Magazine*, 130–133.

Garcia, J., Masol. V., Goossens, S. and Schoutens, W. (2009). Lévy base correlation. *Wilmott Journal 2*.

Geske, R. (1977). The valuation of corporate liabilities as compound options. *Journal of Financial and Quantitative Analysis*, **12**, 541–552.

Geske, R. (1979). The valuation of compound options. *Journal of Financial Economics*, **7**, 63–81.

Grigelionis, B. (1999) Processes of Meixner type. *Lithuanian Mathematical Journal*, **39** (1), 33–41.

Guégan, D. and Houdain, J. (2005). Collateralized Debt Obligations pricing and factor models: a new methodology using Normal Inverse Gaussian distributions. Note de Recherche IDHE-MORA No. 007-2005, ENS Cachan.

Hilberink, B. and Rogers, L. (2002). Optimal capital structure and endogenous default. *Finance and Stochastics*, **6**, 237–263.

Hirsa, A. and Madan, D. (2003). Pricing American options under variance gamma. *Journal of Computational Finance*, **7**.

Hooda, S. (2006). *Explaining base correlation skew using Normal-Gamma process.* Technical Report, Nomura Securities International.

Hull, J. and White, A. (2003). The valuation of credit default swap options. *Journal of Derivatives*, **10**, 40–50.

Jarrow, R. and Turnbull, S. (1995). Pricing derivative on financial securities subject to credit risk. *Journal of Finance*, **50**, 53–86.

Jönsson, H. and Schoutens, W. (2008). Single name credit default swaptions meet single-sided jump models. *Review of Derivatives Research*, **11** (1), 153–169.

Jönsson, H. and Schoutens, W. (2009). Pricing constant maturity credit default swaps under jump dynamics. *The Journal of Credit Risk* (to appear).

Jönsson, H., Schoutens, W. and Van Damme, G. (2009). Modeling default and prepayment using Lévy processes: an application to asset-backed securities, *Radon Series on Computational and Applied Mathematics*, **8**.

Kalemanova, A., Schmid, B. and Werner, R. (2007) The Normal Inverse Gaussian distribution for synthetic CDO pricing. *Journal of Derivatives*, **14** (3), 80493.

Karatzas, I. and Shreve, S. (1999). *Brownian Motion and Stochastic Calculus.* Springer.

Kim, I., Ramaswamy, K. and Sundaresan, S. (1993). Does default risk in coupon affect the valuation of corporate bonds? A contingent claim model. *Financial Management*, **22**, 117–131.

Kou, S. and Wang, H. (2003). First passage times of a jump diffusion process. *Advances in Applied Probability*, **35**, 504–531.

Kou, S. and Wang, H. (2004). Option pricing under a double exponential jump-diffusion model. *Management Science*, **50**, 1178–1192.

Kyprianou, A. (2006). *Introductory Lectures on Fluctuations of Lévy Processes with Applications.* Springer-Verlag, Berlin.

Kyprianou, A. and Surya, B. (2007). Principles of smooth and continuous fit in the determination of endogenous bankruptcy levels. *Finance and Stochastics*, **11**, 131–152.

Lando, D. (1998), On Cox Processes and Credit Risky Securities, *Review of Derivatives Research*, **2** (2-3), 99–120.

Leland, H. (1994). Corporate debt value, bond convenants, and optimal capital structure. *Journal of Finance*, **49**, 1213–1252.

Leland, H. and Toft, K. (1996). Optimal capital structure, endogenous bankruptcy, and the term structure of credit spreads. *Journal of Finance*, **51**, 987–1019.

Leoni, P. and Schoutens, W. (2008). Multivariate smiling. *Wilmott Magazine*, March, 82–91.

Li, A. (1995), A one-factor lognormal Markovian interest rate model: theory and implementation, *Advances in Futures and Options Research*, **8**.

Lipton, A. (2002). Assets with jumps. *Risk*, September, 149–153.

Longstaff, F. and Schwartz, E. (1995). Corporate debt value, bond convenants, and optimal capital structure. *Journal of Finance*, **50**, 789–819.

Luciano, E. and Schoutens, W. (2006). A multivariate jump-driven financial asset model. *Quantitative Finance*, **6** (5), 385–402.

Madan, D., Carr, P. and Chang, E. (1998). The variance–gamma process and option pricing. *European Finance Review*, **2**, 79–105.

Madan, D. and Milne, F. (1991). Option pricing with v.g. martingale components. *Mathematical Finance*, **1**, 39–55.

Madan, D. and Schoutens, W. (2008). Break on through to the single side. *Journal of Credit Risk*, **4** (3), 3–20.

Madan, D. and Seneta, E. (1987). Chebyshev polynomial approximations and characteristic function estimation. *Journal of the Royal Statistical Society Series B*, **49**, 163–169.

Madan, D. and Seneta, E. (1990). The v.g. model for share market returns. *Journal of Business*, **63**, 511–524.

Mandelbrot, B.B. and Taylor, H.M. (1967). On the distribution of stock price differences. *Operations Research*, **15**, 1057–1062.

Masol, V. and Schoutens, W. (2007) *Comparing some alternative Lévy base correlation models for pricing and hedging CDO tranches*. Technical Report 08-01, Section of Statistics, K.U. Leuven.

Mazataud, P. and Yomtov, C. (2000). *The Lognormal method applied to ABS analysis*. Moody's Special Report.

McGinty, L., Beinstein, E., Ahluwalia, R. and Watts, M. (2004). Introducing base correlation. *Technical Report JPMorgan, Credit Derivatives Strategy*.

Merton, R. (1974). On the pricing of corporate debt: the risk structure of interest rates. *Journal of Finance*, **29**, 449–470.

Michael, J., Schucany, W. and Haas, R. (1976). Generating random variates using transformation with multiple roots. *The American Statistician*, **30**, 88–90.

Moosbrucker, T. (2006). *Pricing CDOs with correlated variance gamma distributions*. Research Report, Department of Banking, University of Cologne.

Nicolato, E. and Venardos, E. (2003). Option pricing in stochastic volatility models of the Ornstein–Uhlenbeck type. *Mathematical Finance*, **13**, 445–466.

Nomura Fixed Income Research (2005). *Constant maturity CDS – a guide*. Technical Report, Nomura Securities International.

Nowell, P. (2008). *Asset-Backed Credit Derivatives: Products, Applications and Markets*. Risk Books, London.

O'Kane, D. and Livasey, M. (2004) Base correlation explained. *Quantitative Credit Research Quarterly*, **2004-Q3/4** Lehman Brothers.

Pederson, C.M. (2004) Introduction to credit default swaptions. *Quantitative Credit Research Quarterly*, **2004-Q3/4.7**. Lehman Brothers.

Raynes, S. and Rutledge, A. (2003), *The Analysis of Structured Securities: Precise Risk Measurement and Capital Allocation*, Oxford University Press.

Richards, F.J. (1959), A flexible growth function for empirical use. *Journal of Experimental Botany*, **10**, (2), 290–300.

Rogers, L.C.G. (2000). Evaluating first-passage probabilities for spectrally one-sided Lévy processes. *Journal of Applied Probability*, **37**, 1173–1180.

Rogozin, B. (1996). On distributions of functionals related to boundary problems for processes with independent increments. *Theory of Probability and its Applications*, **11**, 580–591.

Sato, K. (1999). *Lévy Processes and Infinitely Divisible Distributions*. Cambridge Studies in Advanced Mathematics 68, Cambridge University Press, Cambridge.

Sato, K., Watanabe, T. and Yamazato, M. (1994). Recurrence conditions for multidimensional processes of Ornstein–Uhlenbeck type. *Journal of Mathematical Society of Japan*, **46**, 245–265.

Sato, K. and Yamazato, M. (1982). Stationary processes of Ornstein–Uhlenbeck type. In K. Itō and J. Prohorov (eds), Probability Theory and Mathematical Statistics, Vol. 1021 of *Lecture Notes in Mathematics*. Birkhäuser, Boston.

Schoutens, W. (2002) *Meixner processes: theory and applications in finance*. EURANDOM Report 2002-004, EURANDOM, Eindhoven.

Schoutens, W. (2003). *Lévy Processes in Finance: Pricing Financial Derivatives*. John Wiley, & Sons Ltd.

Schönbucher, P.J. (2003), *Credit Derivatives Pricing Models*, Wiley Finance.

Seneta, E. (2007). The early years of the variance-gamma process. In R.J. Elliott *et al.* (eds), *Advances in Mathematical Finance*. Birkhäuser.

Tompkins, R. and Hubalek, F. (2000). *On closed form solutions for pricing options with jumping volatility*. Unpublished Paper.

Uzun, H. and Webb, E. (2007), Securitization and risk: empirical evidence on US banks, *The Journal of Risk Finance*, **8**, (1), 11–23.

Vasicek, O. (1987). *Probability of loss on loan portfolio*. Technical Report, KMV Corporation.

Wolfe, S. (1982). On a continuous analogue of the stochastic difference equation $\rho x_{n+1} + b_n$. *Stochastic Processes and Their Applications*, **12**, 301–312.

Zhou, C. (1996). *A jump-diffusion approach to modelling credit risk and valuing defaultable securities*. Technical Report, Federal Reserve Board, Washington.

Zhou, C. (2001). The term structure of credit spreads with jump risk. *Journal of Banking and Finance*, **25**, 2015–2040.

Index

Index compiled by Terry Halliday
(HallidayTerence@aol.com)